ROMANIAN INVITATION

D1327014

Romanian Invitation

WILLIAM FORWOOD

Garnstone Press

Romanian Invitation
is published by
THE GARNSTONE PRESS LIMITED
59 *Brompton Road, London* S.W.3
SBN: 900391 17 0

© William Forwood 1968
Printed by Balding + Mansell, London & Wisbech

FOREWORD

Romania is a country we are all going to hear a lot more about. Partly for pleasure, because it is certain to become in the '70's one of the great new European tourist centres: partly because it has an individuality, and a place in any European scheme of things, all its own. On the material plane, it has immense natural resources, rather like France. In other ways too, people have often called it the France of Eastern Europe, and that is rather more than a rhetorical flourish. The cultural links with France have always been strong. Read *Secolul* 20, the excellent Bucharest literary monthly, and you will see how strong those links remain. I very much hope that we can develop similar ties with our own country.

In fact, Romania is unique. It lies in the heartland of Slavonic Europe, but it is quite different from the Slav countries – and I can say that, since I know the Slavs and love them. The Roman legions left their own Latin language in Romania, the most remote Latin outpost of the empire. They left more than that. To this day, Romania not only speaks a language very much like Italian, but has a population which possesses the sparkle, the intelligence, the physical appearance that one meets in Tuscany and the Lombard plain. In the long run they have everything – natural riches, great scenic variety, wide-spread education, gifted people – which will make for a brilliant future.

Mr. William Forwood has written an enticing introduction to Romania, designed for English readers to whom it is still mysterious. He writes with heart-felt enthusiasm: he loves every square metre of Romanian soil, from the Dracula country down to the wild marshes of the Danube mouths. The more English people read him, and then are moved to follow in his tracks, the better for everyone. The only way to appreciate a country is to go and live there. A fortnight isn't much, but it is better than nothing. We want Romanians to come and visit us, and English people to visit them, preferably with Mr. Forwood's book somewhere near to hand.

C. P. SNOW 7.8.68

CONTENTS

7

INDEX TO ILLUSTRATIONS

PHOTOGRAPHS

Between page 16 and page 17
1. The Europa Hotel at Eforie Nord on the Black Sea.
2. Bran Castle, near Braşov.
3. Camping Site at Tuşnad.
4. General view of the beach at Mamaia.

Between page 48 and page 49
5. The Sports Hotel at Poiana Braşov.
6. The Village Museum in Bucharest.
7. Landscape in the Apuseni Mountains.
8. The Suceviţa Monastery in Northern Moldavia.

Between page 80 and page 81
9. Another view of the Suceviţa Monastery.
10. The 'Pietrele Doamnei' in the Rarău Mountains.
11 The ruins of Histria, a 7th century B.C. Greek citadel.
12. The Savings and Deposit Bank in Bucharest.

Between page 112 and page 113
13. Peleş Castle at Sinaia.
14. A view of the Olt Valley.
15. The Prahova Valley, highway to the East.
16. The Bicaz Gorges in the Oriental Carpathians.

MAPS

Romania, page 12
Bucharest and Wallachia, page 24
The Dobrogea, page 46
Moldavia, page 64
Transylvania, page 78
The Banat and Oltenia, page 102

CHAPTER ONE

Romania Today

A GENERAL AND PRACTICAL INTRODUCTION

Geography and topography – General history – Novelty of a Romanian visit – Travel and tourism – Accommodation and restaurants – Romanian cooking and wines – Climate – Spas and health resorts — National Tourist Offices – Six main provinces treated in subsequent chapters.

There is no country in Europe so rewarding on first acquaintance. A land whose ancient towns, majestic mountains and pastoral countryside bear witness to an illustrious and individual history, a land of infinite visual charm and human hospitality, a land now transforming itself into a modern society ready and able to compete with other nations for the attention of the foreign traveller.

Romania possesses novelty, she shows a diversity of landscape, folk traditions and art; she is welcoming and accessible and offers multitudinous comforts and pleasures of the table. Every season shows the Romanian countryside to good advantage, whether sun-filled days on the bright sands of the Black Sea or an autumnal vision of apple-trees heavy with fruit, be it the wintry glitter of Carpathian ski-slopes or in spring, the throb of new life in the vast forests and the swell of rivers teeming with fish. And the cities and towns, spas and seaside resorts, the countless monuments – from Greek Histria to modern Bucharest – even the remotest villages tucked away in mountain valleys, exert a perennial attraction.

Situated in the middle of South-Eastern Europe, Romania shares certain characteristics with her Balkan and Central European neighbours but at the same time preserves a highly individualistic civilisation and a physical aspect which has no parallel in Europe.

Romania extends some 300 miles from north to south, and 400 miles from east to west. In the north and north-east she has common frontiers with the USSR, to the west and south-west with Hungary and Yugoslavia, and to the south with Bulgaria. Facing east are 150 miles of coastline. The Danube forms a natural boundary to the south while the River Pruth separates Romania from Soviet Moldavia.

A variety of landscapes correspond to the relief of the country, to the different climatic conditions and vegetation and to the distinctive cultural traditions of the Romanian people. The most striking features of this landscape are the Carpathian Mountains which sweep from north to south-west in a great rectangular chain, and the broad plains which mark the river basins of the Danube and Pruth. Between these extremes, however, there is a rippling succession of wooded foothills and fertile plateaux. In fact a tripartite division into plains, hills and mountains completes the symmetry of this diamond-shaped country, for at its very centre rises Moldoveanu (8,346 feet), the highest peak of the Romanian Carpathians. Several other summits approach this height, but they are scattered unevenly along the whole chain, from the Rodna and Caliman Massifs in the north to the Bucegi and Făgăraş Ranges in central Romania to the Retezat Mountains in the west. Numerous defiles such as the magnificent gorge of the Danube known as the Iron Gates, the steep valleys of the Olt and Prahova Rivers and the Bicaz Gap in Moldavia provide natural gateways through the high ridges.

On the eastern flanks of the Carpathians lies Moldavia and to south, reaching all the way to the Danube, Wallachia. These were the two historic principalities united in 1859 as the new Romania. In the north western part of the country, inside the sweeping arc of mountains, lies the great plateau of Transylvania, an agricultural heartland of gentle undulations and wide valleys watered by rivers such as the Mureş and Someş. Transylvania, after centuries of Austro-Hungarian rule, was finally united with Romania in 1918.

To complete the overall picture, mention should be made of two plains at the western and eastern extremities of the country, the Banat and Dobrogea respectively. The Banat, whose river basin extends into Yugoslavia and Hungary, shared the same history as Transylvania. The Dobrogea, on the other hand, spread between the Danube and the Black Sea, has a character all its own thanks to its maritime traditions and the extraordinary physical composition of the Danube delta region, unique in Europe. Long under Turkish occupation, it was united to Romania in 1878, by the terms of the Berlin Congress.

From the west European, especially an English viewpoint, Romania until recently appeared remote and inaccessible and for this reason was too little known. While there is considerable novelty in a journey there, Romania is as easily reached as any other country in Europe.

Air routes connect in Bucharest with the principal cities of Western and Eastern Europe; through trains run between Romania's cities and several points in the west such as Vienna, Munich, Berlin and Paris; steamers ply from Constanţa to several Black Sea ports, including Istanbul.

Inside the country, a system of new, well-surfaced and notably uncongested roads, a tight rail network and air links between all the main towns and resorts make travel a real pleasure. Romantics may be attracted to the small dusty lanes which wind through the wooded countryside and equally to the rural steam locomotives shining in their bright paint and polished brass, but realists appreciate that the Romanian government is currently pursuing a rapid course of modernisation in travel and tourism, as in every other field. The country's present five-year plan provides for 53,000 more beds, 3,000 miles of highway modernisation, a new motorway from Bucharest to Piteşti, with an ultimate extension to the west, the first road in the Delta region, a massive bridge across the Danube to replace the ferry at Giurgeni, a modern highway at the Iron Gates, an Intercontinental Hotel and the construction of several new resorts on the Black Sea. Such developments anticipate many more foreign visitors than the 1967 figure of 1½ million would suggest. For all the changes of the near future, Romania is as easy to visit today, whether one goes alone or in a group. Entry regulations are minimal (citizens of the UK and US can obtain visas at the borders), internal travel is fast and convenient and accommodations are more than ample.

All towns have traditional-style but comfortable hotels, while the larger cities and resorts maintain hotels of the highest international standards. In this class may be recommended the following: *Bucharest*, Athénée Palace, Lido (with terrace and swimming pool), Ambasador, Nord, Union and Victoria; *Băile Herculane*, Cerna; *Braşov*, Carpaţi (probably the most luxurious in the country); *Cluj*, Continental; *Craiova*, Minerva; *Jassy*, Continental: *Oradea*, Transylvania; *Piatra Neamţ*, Ceahlau; *Predeal*, Rosmarin; *Sibiu*, Imparatul Romanilor; *Sinaia*, Palas; *Suceava*, Central; *Timişoara*, Banatul. On the coast, particularly at *Mamaia, Eforie Nord, Eforie Sud* and *Mangalia*, there are many, such as the Europa in *Eforie Nord* which are of the first order, most of them ultramodern. At the new coastal resort of *Neptun* there is a complex of hotels which deserve to win several prizes for the elegance and spirit of their architecture. Over 100 recognised camping grounds set in attractive surroundings near major towns and resorts make for informal holidays; tourist huts and chalets, especially in the Southern Carpathians, give shelter to walkers and climbers and a growing number of motels and tourist inns done in Romanian village style sustain the motorist on main highways.

1. The Europa Hotel at Eforie Nord on the Black Sea.

2. Bran Castle, near Braşov.

3. *right:* Camping Site at Tuşnad.

4. General view of the beach at Mamaia.

Good restaurants abound in every part of the country. Amongst the most famous are the 'Miorița' at Mamaia; the 'Băneasa' in the Forest of Băneasa outside Bucharest and 'Cerbul Carpatin' at Brașov. These and many others show Romanian cuisine to its best advantage.

The pleasures of the Romanian kitchen are very special. An unlimited variety of meats, fish, game, vegetables, fruit, herbs and spices makes for as succulent and distinctive a range of dishes as may be found in Europe. Without compiling an inventory of the many regional specialities, the following selection is representative of the country at large. Breakfasts comprise more than the continental roll and coffee; they can include omelettes and various meats. Lunch and dinner can start with a goose-liver pâté or one of several sweet-sour soups, *ciorba de perisoare* (a thick paysanne type with meat-balls and vegetables, often highly spiced) or *ciorba de potroace* (made from giblets) or the rich *borshch de miel* containing lamb and sometimes garnished with eggs and cream. The meal will continue with *ghiveciu*, a thick and savoury vegetable stew, *tocane*, a meat stew based on beef or pork and flavoured with spices and onions, with *ardei umpluti* (stuffed peppers) or the Moldavian rissole of spiced minced meat known as *pîrjoala*. *Patricieni* (grilled sausage, highly seasoned) and *mititei* (grilled sausages) are also popular. More exotic are *piftie* (seasoned pork in aspic), *pastrama* (smoked goat meat) and the innumerable preparations of venison, especially delicious in Transylvania. In the Delta, cooks excel at roasting fresh carp on spits; in Oltenia and most mountain areas a host of recipes for the preparation of freshwater fish are to be found. The above-mentioned dishes will be accompanied by vegetables and salads of excellent quality, many of them novel to northern tastes, juicy, earth-rich tomatoes and eggplants, sharply flavoured peppers and gherkins and a wide choice of fruit according to season; water melon, cherries, apples, grapes, quince. A national favourite, if not a staple food, is *mamaliga*, a kind of polenta, which is company for many meals such as *sarmale* (the famous stuffed cabbage or vine leaves) or simply for egg dishes. Cream, yogurt, small green peppers add piquancy to these courses.

To sweeten the palate at the end of dinner, several sumptous desserts are offered: the universal *plăcinte* (turnovers with various fillings) and *cozonac* (a brioche, particularly good in Moldavia); *halva, baclava* (nuts and honey) and *cataif* (whipped cream), all of which are Turkish in origin, excellent ice-cream and, notably in Transylvania, a wealth of patisserie.

Of their wines, Romanians are rightly boastful. These derive from many districts and vary accordingly. The best vineyards must include *Cotnari* (celebrated especially for its Feteasca and Arasa wines), *Murfatlar* (Rieslings, Chardonnay, Pinot Negru and Muscats), *Niculitel* (Băbeasca), *Tîirnave* (dry Riesling and a fragrant light perla), *Sadova* (Rosé), and *Southern Transylvania* (Muscat Otonel). Romanian champagnes, particularly the *Zarea* variety, are outstanding.

In the autumn large tankards of *must*, unfermented wines fresh from the vineyards, are available at the many *mustării* which spring up by the roadside as part of the harvest festivities.

It would be hard not to mention the good beer and the ubiquitous *ţuica* or plum brandy which enlivens the beginning of many a meal. Romanian coffee is made in Turkish fashion and has a more agreeable consistency than in other Balkan countries. The tea is weak. Whisky, gin and spirits imported from abroad are obtained at hotels and restaurants in the chief cities and resorts.

The climate of Romania is one of continental extremes tempered at times by transitional factors. The first official day of spring (1st March) often falls when snow remains upon the ground, the so-called 'lambs' snow' coming at lambing time. Then equally in late autumn, when the sun still hangs high at midday, the lilacs may suddenly bloom in a kind of Indian summer. The real summer is more predictable: constant heat and sunshine relieved by occasional showers, and in winter you can be sure to welcome the warmth of indoor stoves and wood fires and the cheerful glow of lights as snow covers plain and mountain. All seasons are good for travel, though the coast is at its best in the summer months, and the Carpathian ski-resorts in the late winter. Large cities, particularly Bucharest, have year-round attractions, and the seasonal cycle of nature makes such centres of wild life as the Danube Delta or Retezat National Park fascinating in every month.

Romania's new seaside resorts are justly famous; her spas, some of them visited in Classical days, remain surprisingly less known. These are of three kinds. Along the Black Sea shore salty lagoons, the landlocked remains of ancient arms of the sea, contain rich deposits of mud with therapeutic properties. Most famous is Lake Tekirghiol with its mud baths, salt baths, its lake bathing and the famous nearby beach resorts of Eforie Nord and Eforie Sud. The presence of the sea and a climate as magnificent as any in Europe provide a perfect setting for the treatment of various ailments, including diseases of the nervous and locomotor systems, blood diseases, rheumatism and gynaecological complaints.

Further inland on the Danubian Plain the retreating sea left in the pre-historic era a residue of salt pools. One such is at Amara which lies not far from the main road between the capital and the coast. Its salty and radioactive waters have exceptional curative powers in severe cases of rheumatism.

It is in the Carpathians, however, where the greatest number of spas may be found. Some 2,000 mineral springs bubble from underground streams and wells along the entire extent of what is the longest volcanic chain in Europe. The fresh and effervescent mountain air makes such resorts as Tuşnad, Călimăneşti and Govora, along the Olt River, and Băile Herculane, Băile Felix and Sovata (to name but a few) elsewhere, beautiful places in their own right, but the extraordinary wealth and variety of mineral waters, sulphurous, sodium chloric, calcic, carbonic and magnesic, combine to offer an unparalleled assortment of cures for several ailments.

As a major industry, tourism is actively promoted by the Romanians themselves and there are Romanian National Tourist Offices in London (99 Jermyn Street, s.w.1), Paris, Brussels, Vienna, Frankfurt, Rome, Copenhagen, Stockholm, New York, in Bucharest (7 Boulevard Magheru, at the airport and Gara de Nord) and at all principal towns in Romania. For the foreigner the NTO organises accommodation, excursions and currency exchange and is an invaluable source of information.

The chapters that follow divide the country into sections which, it is hoped, the visitor should find manageable. Romania contains surprising contrasts, in scenery and culture alike; the Black Sea coast, the saw-like outlines of the Retezat Mountains, the hustle and bustle of Bucharest are, to the eye at least, worlds apart, but travel is so simple that it is by no means difficult to fit several distinctive regions into one itinerary. The road or railway traveller arriving from Hungary or Yugoslavia and destined for the Black Sea resorts or Bucharest can, without adding hugely to his mileage, include a number of unusual places almost totally undiscovered by the western tourist yet not remote or inaccessible. The compact shape and, for the most part, common frontiers with other states, make Romania a country without a John o' Groats or Alaska. Probably the least visited regions are the Banat and Oltenia, not on account of their distance from Western Europe – from England, for instance, they lie close to the shortest route to Bucharest – but simply because too little is known about them. For many motorists with scarce time at their disposal it may be difficult to venture far beyond the Transylvanian cities of Cluj or Tîrgu Mureş, but a slight détour could easily encompass the beautiful painted churches and rolling countryside of northern Moldavia.

Wallachia (Chapter 2), as one of the three historic principalities, possesses three old cities: Curtea de Argeş, Cîmpulung and Tîrgovişte which are to Romania what Segovia and Toledo are to Spain, or Cracow to Poland. Bucharest, with all the amenities of a capital city and many characteristic monuments from several centuries, is the pulse and pacesetter of a fast changing nation, but its countryside is still a golden granary interspersed with forests and rivers; the southern Carpathians are so close that no one visiting Bucharest should miss a trip to the mountain resorts and spas of the Prahova Valley, gateway to Transylvania. Likewise the region known as the Dobrogea (Chapter 3), with some of the best beaches in Europe, important classical sites and the unequalled wild life of the Danube Delta, is within easy access.

The other principal regions are further from the capital but, on the other hand, nearer to the Hungarian, Yugoslav and Soviet frontier points which the northern visitor is most likely to cross. Moldavia (Chapter 4), for so long a province known to West Europeans only through their history books stands on the brink of change and yet the almost nostalgic serenity of its pastoral and mountain scenery, unchanged for centuries, will never, as the larger cities have done, yield to the pressures of industrialisation. Its painted churches are, without a doubt, one of the greatest expressions of anonymous art in the world.

Though not a part of the 'Old Kingdom' of Romania which had existed before the First World War, Transylvania (Chapter 5) abounds in the Romantic associations and extravagant forms of nature which readers of Dracula expect of Romania, just as Scotland so amply rewards the devotees of the legendary Ossian. The old cities of Braşov, Sighişoara and Sibiu resemble scenes depicted by 17th- and 18th-century lithographers and the theatrical castles of Bran and Hunedoara, the angular wooden churches of Maramureş surpass all expectations.

The last two regions, the Banat and Oltenia (Chapter 6), treated here as one for the sake of convenience, are in some respects a microcosm of the rest of the country: the richly cultivated plains of the Banat, the Arcadian gentleness of the sylvan slopes of the River Olt, the Iron Gates – a river gorge as stupendous as any between the Yangtze and Colorado – or the shadow of Rome at Băile Herculane; these are quintessentially a part of the lavish and, to western eyes, exotic heritage of Romania.

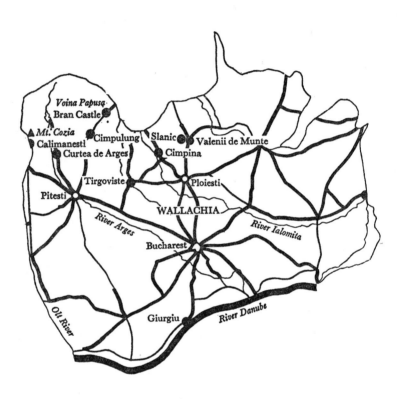

CHAPTER TWO

Bucharest and Wallachia

Arrival at Bucharest – First impressions – History –
Architectural influences – Brancovan style – Capital of Romania
since 1862 – 19th-century efflorescence – 20th- century unrest –
N.T.O. – Scînteia – Herăstrău Park and Village Museum –
Minovici Museum – Athenaeum – Art Museum – Modern centre –
Piaţa Unirii – Grand National Assembly and Patriarchate –
Several churches – Russian Museum – National Museum of
Antiquities – Stadium – Cişmigiu Gardens – Night Life –
Environs of city: Mogoşoaia, Snagov and forests – Old Wallachia:
Ploieşti, Slănic, Tîrgovişte, Cîmpulung, Curtea de Argeş.

The name Bucharest, Bucarest, Bukarest, in Romanian
Bucureşti, evokes the palmy days of leisurely railway journeys
across the Ruritanian map of Europe, and it is perhaps surprising to find in modern Bucharest a city very much of the
20th century, containing one and a half million inhabitants,
one fifth of Romania's industry and her most important cultural institutions. The main road from the Carpathians enters
the city from the north skirting the Forest of Băneasa and the
International Airport, and leads into the spacious Chaussée
Kisseleff. By train, however, the night traveller is awoken by
the Romanian train attendant just as the fugitive vision of
maize fields ripening in the Wallachian plain gives way to the
outlying farms and kitchen gardens, then to the new suburbs
of gleaming white masonry until finally the train draws to a
standstill in the Gara de Nord, a bright, spotless and capa-
cious station whose flower-beds and pots of scarlet geraniums

seem to extend an unspoken welcome to the stranger. Romanians seated at tables on the platform are already breakfasting on sauerkraut, smoked sausage and thick coffee; placards announce the destinations of trains . . . Paris . . . Budapest . . . Warsaw, and the dust of the morning dances in the shafts of sunlight.

The first impression of the capital is one of spaciousness and trees. Everywhere planes, limes, willows and poplars give shade and a visual relief from the broad and blinding stretches of roadway. Much of the centre of the city is post-war and ultra-modern, white clean and functional, but the 19th-century geometrical plan has not been abandoned; wide chaussées and avenues reminiscent of Haussmann criss-cross by way of vast circular intersections in which statuary, foliage and fountains provide a refreshing focus. The more recent the buildings, the more streamlined and translucent their look. By contrast the neo-Baroque and often whimsical architecture pre-dating the First World War, very much in evidence along the boulevards radiating from the centre, has a grandeur of proportion and elaborateness of detail entirely characteristic of its age, relaxed and opulent if doubtless less efficient than its successor styles.

Though possessing an ancient history which stretches back to palaeolithic times, Bucharest was first mentioned in a text by Prince Vlad the Impaler who, in 1459, built a fortress here on the sluggish River Dîmbovița as part of a network of defences designed to assist the protection of the Wallachian hinterland from Turkish invasion. The new settlement was, according to legend, named after a shepherd called Bucur. During subsequent centuries Bucharest developed as a focal point of trade between Central Europe and Constantinople and as the chief centre of the fertile plains. The more northerly cities of Cîmpulung, Curtes de Argeş and Tirgovişte, well girded by mountains and therefore less vulnerable, had served till the late Middle Ages as the princely capitals of Wallachia (also called Muntenia), but the princes also maintained an alternate seat in Bucharest and in 1659 the city became the official capital of the principality. Around the court grew up boyars' houses surrounded by gardens and vineyards and famous inns named after their rich proprietors: Manuc, Serban Vodă, Crețulescu, arcaded buildings with huge inner courtyards sheltering the merchants' carts. Of these only Manuc's inn has remained and it has been recently restored in the original style.

By the early 19th century Bucharest had acquired a large number of churches and schools and had played a central rôle in the country's history, in the 1655 revolts of Wallachian bodyguards and infantry, in the 1764 uprising of the guilds, in Tudor Vladimirescu's insurrection of 1821 and most of all, in the great and contagious upheavals of 1848 when Nicolae Bălcescu, one of the fathers of the Romanian nation, proclaimed a revolutionary constitution for Wallachia. The Turks reacted brutally by massacring a brave but outnumbered insurgent company of the fire brigade on a hill known as Dealul Spirei. Bălcescu, Ana Ipătescu, General Magheru and other leaders of the revolt were exiled but gave their names to three of today's major thoroughfares.

The autonomy of the Romanian principalities minimised the Turkish impact on the culture of Wallachia and Moldavia and there was never in Bucharest the medley of minarets and madrassehs found in the Ottoman cities of Sofia, Salonika or Sarajevo. Houses were usually of wood and therefore prone to catch fire; the Turks on several occasions burned parts of the city and the Great Fire of 1847 was especially catastrophic. As a result the oldest extant buildings, mainly churches and palaces, dating from the 16th, 17th and 18th centuries, are solid structures of brick and stone. Byzantine influences were at first strong, as may be seen in the Church of the Curtea Veche (Old Palace), in the Patriarchate and at the Fundenii Doamnei Church in the north-eastern suburb of Colentina. At the same time the great height of these churches was quite foreign to Byzantium and much of their decoration suggests Georgian, Armenian or Persian inspiration. At the Fundenii Doamnei Church, built in 1699 by Prince Michael Cantacuzino, the stucco of the exterior walls shows strong affinities with the East but the spirit of all these buildings is distinctive and individual, prophetic of a kind of Romanian Renaissance. A truly Wallachian style was, indeed, soon crystallised in the work of the Brancovan period, named after Prince Constantin Brîncoveanu (1688–1714) whose supreme monuments are the Palace at Mogoşoaia and the monastery of Hurez in Oltenia but whose impact on his country was by no means restricted to the realm of art. In Bucharest proper the best Brancovan buildings include the Stavro-poleos Church built by Mihail Cantacuzino on the site of an older edifice, the Creţulescu Church, the work (1722) of a son-in-law of Brîncoveanu and the historic Church of St. George, built in 1670 by Brîncoveanu himself and later to house his mortal remains. The principal characteristics of the Brancovan style are a symmetrical plan, delicate arcades and porticoes with supporting columns of stone, and ogival arches traced with an elaborate profusion of floral and geo-metric motifs. The churches are often crowned by small and somewhat stunted cupolas but the two towers of the Creţu-lescu Church are untypically tall and topped with domes, again suggestive of Caucasian influence. The frescoes, partic-ularly in the latter church, are excellent.

The repeated ravages of fire, earthquakes, plague and the Turkish invasions encouraged a gradual and systematic re-planning of the city and General Kisseleff, whose liberal gov-ernorship of the principalities followed Russian victories over the Turks in 1829, presided over major improvements. Then in 1848 the uprisings against Turkish rule involved street battles and brought ruthless retaliation from the Ottoman cavalry. The importance of Bucharest was enhanced in 1856 when both Wallachia and Moldavia were declared autonom-ous principalities, a major concession won at the Congress of Paris. Three years later, in 1859, both principalities elected

Alexandra Ioan Cuza as their joint Prince and were named the United Principalities. While the Moldavian capital of Jassy (Iaşi) had substantial claim to be the capital of the union, the strategic and commercial significance of Bucharest proved decisive. Thus in 1862 the city became the capital of Romania and in 1878 the new state gained full sovereignty following the Russo-Romanian rout of the Turkish armies. The names of certain streets such as Calea Victoriei, Calea Griviţtei and Calea Plevnei commemorate this War of Independence.

Bucharest now grew conscious of its rôle as a European capital; wealth from burgeoning business and industry stimulated the city's expansion; the new Orient Express and Danubian steamers brought the 'Paris of the Balkans' within reach of Western Europe. In a city which had traditionally supported great numbers of Greeks, Turks, Bulgarians, Jews, Armenians, Russians and others, there developed a culture, both national and cosmopolitan that was the envy of South East Europe. Mansions and villas of the utmost elegance were set at generous intervals along the parks and boulevards to accommodate the aristocracy and rich merchants; their style was florid and expressed a new composite art from which architects such as Ion Mincu (1851–1912) evolved on the basis of Wallachian and Moldavian traditions. Mincu restored many buildings such as the Stavropoleos Church and carried their essence over into his own creations, such as the Central Lycée, The People's Council Building and the restaurant on the Chaussée known as the Buffet (Bufetul). Garden terraces and watering places dotted the metropolis and they remain today for the enjoyment of everybody.

The First World War brought destruction and disorder to the Romanian capital; in 1917, when Bucharest was under German occupation, there were echoes of the two Russian Revolutions and in the following year mass demonstrations and strikes provoked a reign of terror and over one hundred demonstrators were mown down outside the National

Theatre. Between the wars further monuments fittings to a capital were erected, and the city's confines expanded. This, however, was a period of great unrest, in Romania as elsewhere in Central and Eastern Europe, and in 1933 thousands of oil and railway workers staged a massive strike, known as the Grivița Roşie uprising, drawing much fire and blood. Then, in the latter years of the Second World War, the country's reversal of alliances brought in its train street fighting and German air bombardments which damaged not only housing but also several institutions such as the Romanian Atheneum, the National Theatre and University.

After the Second World War the advent of socialist power changed the city's skyline once again. The ovals and volutes of elaborate buildings like the Post Office and the Savings and Deposit Bank which had reflected a turn-of-the-century craze for unrestraint gave way to a style of austere magnificence; new hotels and office blocks and various education establishments bore the impact of functionalism and socialist realism in concrete. Like similar structures in Moscow and Warsaw, the vast Scînteia Buildings, headquarters of the nation's press and publishing, spiked the sky with its crenellated towers and pointed shafts. Much of the central area was rebuilt and the small houses which remained on the Bulevard Gen. Magheru were replaced by the stores, hotels and National Tourist Office of today. By 1960 a distinctly national spirit had re-emerged and since then the ease, lightness and scale of subsequent civic buildings, housing and supermarkets bespeak the enormous confidence which Romanians hold in their future. The new Square of the Palace of the Republic (Piaţa Palatului R.S.R.) and the Calea Griviţiei preserve the open spaces that are so delightful a custom of this city while the new Circus, Radio Concert Hall, National Economic Pavilion and Giuleşti Cinema are the last word in experiment and are remarkably successful as architecture.

Even more than the other cities of Romania the capital is

the fulcrum of change. Traffic surges along the boulevards in rhythm with the lights; carpenters and glaziers inscribe their names on the windowpanes of shining new apartment blocks; the old cobble pavement is fast disappearing, yet life continues and the citizens take time out as they have always done. Ice-cream vendors and summer strollers seek refuge in the flickering shade of the lime trees; conversation and the café life, two favourite entertainments of the Romanian, flourish in the coffee houses and beer gardens.

As in all large cities on first acquaintance you are concerned with finding bearings and then with discovering what is special and different. A bus ride from the centre to Herăstrău Park suggests to the newcomer just how extensive are the stretches of garden, woodland and water in this city. From several points near the multilingual and well-informed National Tourist Office which our visitor can regard as a home-from-home, 19th century avenues radiate in all directions. Those veering north from the Piaţa Victoriei (Victory Square), the Chaussée and Bulevard Aviatorilor (Aviators' Boulevard) extend to the shores of Lakes Herăstrău and Floreasca which form part of the serpentine loop of northern lakes connected by the River Colentina. The top of the Chaussée is dominated by the Scînteia Press Building, from whose summit, say some townspeople, you enjoy the best of panoramas since your view is no longer obstructed by the sugary confection of the Scînteia Building itself. Be that as it may, the breadth of this boulevard and the multitude of great villas and mansions, many housing embassies and other institutions, give a most pleasing impression. The white and yellow stucco of residences set in gardens of fig trees and small loggias recall many Latin cities from Rome to Buenos Aires but the Triumphal Arch, standing halfway up the Chaussée is an echo of Paris.

In Herăstrău Park, a piece of countryside enlivened by a bright mass of flowers and various aquatic sports, is the famous Muzeul Satului (Village Museum) which, amidst its natural landscaping, not only forms an original little village but also gives a real and comprehensive picture of rural life in all the regions of Romania. As in the 'national villages' of Norway and Sweden, this open-air museum displays dwellings, stables, sheds and poultry-houses, summer kitchens and dovecotes, barns and wells, monumental gateways and wickets, stiles, wattle fences, churches and wayside shrines, workshops and rustic working devices – all moved piece by piece from their country settings. They were created for the needs of daily life and, before their removal, used by successive generations. Starting in 1925 with the ethnographical surveys of scholars, the present village has now assembled 291 genuine structures and nearly 20,000 different objects. They vary in shape and colour from house to house and region to region, providing a kaleidoscopic diversity of decoration and incidentally an instructive tour of the country. The effect of this village, its style and spirit, is the more striking if you have just arrived from abroad by air rather than made the overland journey through the pastoral scenery of Transylvania.

Among the oldest homesteads are the 17th-century Zăpodeni house from near Jassy and an early 18th-century dwelling from the village of Chiojdu Mic, near Ploieşti, complete with shaded portico. The continuity in domestic styles is most remarkable, linking present-day rural modes with archaeological materials. The best examples of this are the two 19th-century dug-out huts from Oltenia with characteristic contents, including wreaths of grass, a cock's feathers and wattle for ornamentation, gourds and a neolithic-type dibble. For centuries rural craftsmen have applied similar techniques, whether in the construction of shingle or thatched roofs, or in implements devised for panning gold in the Apuseni Mountains and glazing pottery at Argeş. Walls are covered with decorative ornamental tapestries generally showing geometrical, floral or bird motifs. In the context of Herăstrău, regional distinctions such as the high-pitched straw roofs of homesteads from Bukovina or the low tile roofs of one-storeyed

Dobrogea cottages are obvious to the uninitiated. The tall wooden church from Maramureş, the windmill from the Dobrogea and the many carved gateways from Oltenia and Transylvania are typical of the splendid idioms peculiar to those areas. A sense of timelessness pervades this village, as if the original peasant occupants have merely gone to town for the day. Also in the park are an open-air theatre, swimming pool and the Pescarus restaurant whose leafy terraces overlooks the lake.

More folk arts and artefacts await the enthusiast at the Minovici Museum situated to the west of the park, shortly before the bridge carries traffic across the lake to Băneasa. Dr. Minovici was a noted scientist and connoisseur who in 1936 gave his collection to the nation. In this Mincuesque building, which possesses a Foişor tower, a motif common in sub-Carpathian villages, there are especially fascinating exhibits of icons painted on glass, extraordinary musical instruments, ranging from Transylvanian Alpenhorns to Oltenian bag-pipes, and brilliantly coloured Easter eggs. The practice of painting eggs is found in many Christian countries, but particularly in Eastern Europe, whether Orthodox or Catholic. According to a Romanian legend, the Virgin Mary brought a basket of eggs to be divided among the guards of Jesus on Golgotha in the vain hope of inducing them to pity the sufferings of her son. She laid the basket at the foot of the cross and blood from the divine wounds streamed over the eggs and gave their shells the colour that is used to this day. In fact the egg-shells are first covered with a design of melted wax, then dipped for a moment in a dye, and finally the wax is wiped off with a cloth so that there emerge white patterns on a coloured ground. And, by repeated dippings in different dyes, all kinds of attractive permutations are created.

The Romanians are tireless ethnographers and yet another great collection is displayed in the Museum of Folk Art in the Calea Victoriei, close to the centre of the town.

The narrow twisting Calea Victoriei is the most famous

street of the metropolis and was laid out in the late 18th century by Constantin Brîncoveanu as the main roadway running north to the Palace of Mogoşoaia, one of the chief Brancovan residences. It is lined by a curious jumble of boyar palaces converted into offices, modern blocks of flats, large department stores, the tourist shops Arta Populară and Muzica where handicrafts and music are found and diminutive shops selling paper, boots and groceries, all heavily shuttered against the dazzle of summer. The Athenée Palace Hotel, a cool and grandiose haven of tourists and businessmen, recently enlarged, looks across at the Romanian Athenaeum whose domed rotunda and canary Ionic façade achieve a harmonious compromise between Baroque grandeur and Hellenic grace. This beautiful structure has since 1865 been a traditional mecca of the Romanian musical world and, though surpassed in size by the New Hall of the Palace of the Republic, is still the home of the George Enescu Philharmonic Orchestra, named after the renowned composer and conductor (1881–1955) who was Romania's most accomplished musician. Enescu's life and contribution are also commemorated by the George Enescu Museum (No. 141 Calea Victoriei) in a fine example of the Mincu style done by I. Berindei in 1900.

Returning from the northern end of the Calea Victoriei you will pass on the right the Museum of Art, the country's largest and most representative gallery of national, European and Oriental painting, sculpture, manuscripts, and decorative art. The collection of old masters, housed in some 20 rooms and including good Flemish, Dutch, Venetian and Impressionist work, the Romanian icons and several sculptures by Brancusi deserve the homage of a few hours. And at No. 125 stands the Academy of the Republic whose garden adjoins a vast library containing, in addition to three million books, stamp and coin collections of absorbing interest.

An area to the west of the Calea Victoriei was in 1959 and 1960 totally replanned in a modern but monumental style

34

and in its midst, a large canopied structure reminiscent of the Festival Hall in London was added to the neoclassical Palace of the Republic (formerly the Royal Palace) and is the scene of large congresses and other meetings. Futuristic residential blocks, some of them raised above arcaded shopping precincts, are as much an expression of the mid-20th century as are the international products on sale in the gleaming supermarkets: Pepsi Cola, Queen Anne Whisky, Rice Krispies...

Continue down the Calea Victoriei to the banks of the Dîmboviţa and you approach the Piaţa Unirii, the historic nucleus of Bucharest. Much reconstruction is envisaged for this section, but a number of older monuments are sure of preservation for, in different ways, they embody the spirit of successive ages. Most venerable perhaps is the Stavropoleos Church (Biserica Stavropoleos) built in the 1720's and restored by Mincu, a small gem of the Brancovan style. And Săvulescu's large-scale Post Office (Palutul Poştelor) and Gottereau's Savings and Deposit Bank (Casa de Depuneri) both built in 1900 and recalling Rome's monument to Victor Emmanuel II are equally typical of their time.

Beyond the Piaţa Unirii rises the Hill of the Patriarchate (Dalul Mitropoliei) crowned by two important monuments, the Church of the Patriarchate (Mitropolia) and the Grand National Assembly (Marea Adunare Naţionala). The glossy restoration (1960) of the former may indicate a new building but in fact this church, begun in 1654 by Prince Serban Cantacuzino and closely related to churches at Curtea de Argeş and elsewhere, exemplifies the Wallachian variation on a Byzantine theme. Less ponderous than the churches of Greece or Serbia, its recesses are illuminated by the golden sheen of mural saints and the universal Pancreator. The Grand National Assembly, its long façade broken by a series of neoclassical pilasters, houses the parliament and is unfortunately closed to visitors. The Hill of the Patriarchate is to the citizens of Bucharest what the Bastille and Red Square

are to the populace of other cities and it witnessed, among other events, an uprising against the boyars in 1655 and popular demonstrations for the union of the principalities under Cuza in 1859.

To the west of the hill, behind Splaiul Independenţei, is the Church of Princess Bălaşa (Biserica Domniţa Bălaţa), one of the most elegant churches in the city, built originally in 1751 and named after the daughter of Constantin Brîncoveanu. The present structure dates only from the 1880's but it has interior murals depicting the family of Brîncoveanu and in times of the monarchy, was famous for its choir and magnificent masses.

A good way to regain the modern city centre is to follow the roadway (or the roadworks as may be the case) leading north from the Piaţa Unirii, for there is plenty to see *en route*, but before leaving the vicinity, there are three more, and most rewarding, churches. The Church of St. Spiridion (Biserica Sf. Spiridon), in the Strada Cuza Vodă is the largest church in Bucharest. Built in 1765 by G. Ghica it contains the tombs of many voivods, paintings by the national artist Tattarescu (1820–1894) and a porch carrying a Turkish inscription.

A little further east, on a rise, in the Church of Bucur (Biserica Bucur) which, so the story goes, was first founded in wood by the legendary Bucur. It was later replaced in stone by Mircea the Old, with a tower resembling a shepherd's bonnet. Then there is also the Church of St. Antim (Biserica Antim) built in 1715 and restored. Its founder, the Metropolitan Antim Ivireanu, who may himself have sculpted some of the ornamentation, was an original scholar who clearly admired the austerity and discipline of Moorish and Caucasian styles and there is no denying that the pencil-shaped towers and rigid geometric decoration of his church have affinities with the art of Georgia.

On the southern side of the Piaţa 1848 there once stood the old Prince's court (Curtea Veche) which after countless sackings, fires and earthquakes was irrevocably abandoned in 1775 when Prince Alexandru Ipsilanti moved to a new court close to the monastery of Mihai Vodă. In the golden age of Wallachia this court had been the pivot of the principality's history. A chronicler has described how Constantin Brîncoveanu secured at the outset of his reign the support of the boyars:

> He had the princely house brought to him with all adornments and with all servants, and the entire princely retinue being ready, he mounted and to the Prince's Court in great honour and pomp he went and there he entered, and singing psalms according to custom, the holy icons he kissed and the oath of the boyars accepted who swore by the Holy Gospel to stand with him in righteousness, thence to the princely rooms he went and in the great council chamber he sat on the princely throne and caused the guns to be fired while all the city greatly rejoiced about the new rule that had been inaugurated to the satisfaction of all.

Today only the church remains and, thanks again to restoration, is largely, although in origin the oldest monument in Bucharest, in excellent repair. Its plan is influenced by general features of the three cusped system which one sees to best advantage at the Cozia Monastery in Oltenia where too the ante-nave is covered by a semi-cylindrical vault and the nave crowned by a tower. Despite the regrettable loss of interior frescoes, the logical planning and use of alternating brick and plaster bands in the decoration of the exterior make this a good example of Wallachian church building.

Further along the Bulevard 1848, on the right, is the Colțea Hospital within whose courtyard is the Colțea Church, founded in the early 18th century by Michael Cantacuzino to accompany the Colțea Tower (destroyed in 1888) which had been built by King Charles XII's fugitive soldiers who had found shelter in Bucharest after the Swedish monarch's defeat by Peter the Great at Poltava. One gathers that this was an outstanding landmark. Across the street is the Museum of the History of Bucharest, occupying the former Saţu Palace, in which a wide variety of exhibits document the turbulent history of the capital.

In the Strada Ion Ghica running westward from the Bulevard 1848 is a Russian Church (1906) whose bulbous and multicoloured cupolas are a reminder that, despite Romania's historic association and religious affinities with Russia, the cultures of these countries, here expressed in brick and mortar, are quite different. For the student of Russo-Romanian connections there is an interesting museum, Muzeul Româno-Rus, situated between the Bulevard Gen. Magheru and Calea Victoriei, at No. 4, Strada Fundaţiei. The exhibition traces the interaction of the two countries, from the days when the modern Dobrogea and Ukraine formed ancient Scythia Minor, to the 17th century when Russian craftsmen worked on the Three Hierarchs Church at Jassy, when Romanian Hospodars (Governors) and Russian Princes formed successive alliances, when, in 1670, a Moldavian, Nicolae Milescu, journeyed overland from Moscow to Peking, all the way to the 19th-century quest for Romanian independence and the advent of Communism after the Second World War. The Romanian language was once written in the Cyrillic script; hence the manuscripts and inscriptions that you will see in the older buildings, whether in Romanian or Old Slavonic, shared the same alphabet. And Old Slavonic was to Balkan and Russian orthodoxy what Latin represented to the West.

Not far from the Romanian-Russian collection is the National Museum of Antiquities (No. 11 Strada I.C. Frimu) containing much of archaeological interest. Elsewhere there are further museums devoted to the lives and work of the nation's artists: Storck, Tattarescu, Theodor Aman and others, and several formerly private collections, the most outstanding of which is the Oprescu collection at 16 Strada Dr. Chenet.

Though it is hoped that he was not so foolhardy as to encompass the foregoing in anything less than a few days, our traveller may now be satiated with art and history. Perhaps there is a football match being played at the colossal 23 August Stadium in the eastern part of town; on a fine day the roar of 80,000 devotees of the national game can be exhilarating; conversation with foreigners, in English, French or German, may well turn on the World Cup and the heroics of Bobby Charlton. In this district are many factories, none of them far from the greenery of the Park of 23 August or the gardens along the Colentina River.

The most beautiful of all the city's parks, lies west of the Calea Victoriei, off the Bulevard Gheorghiu-Dej, and is known as the Cişmigiu Garden. A century old, it has the formal lay-out of Latin countries and its topiary and immaculate flower-beds, its study old plane-trees and trembling poplars follow the gentle contour of a hill dominated by the glinting gold cupola of the Schitu Măgureanu Church. Peacocks, like vestiges of a long-lost aristocracy, strut and preen themselves on the scissored lawns.

At night the lights go on and the crowds mingle on the streets. You do not stride; you saunter, taking a cool and frothy beer at the Carul Cu Bere Brasserie in the Strada Stavropoleos or a cocktail on the terraces of the Lido or Athénée Palace Hotels. The Romanians dine late and at considerable length. Of diverse eating-places one of the most charming is the Buffet (Buffetul) off the Chaussée designed by Mincu in the Wallachian manner. Several restaurants, notably the Pădurea Băneasa in the Forest of Băneasa (six miles north) feature folk dancers, singers and gypsy bands where wine and music strike up giddy friendships. The meal should start with a fiery dose of tuica; this arouses an appetite for *gratar* (grilled meat), for *mititei* and other national dishes. It is commendable that the traditional music of this country, often played on special pan-pipes and bagpipes, is still genuinely popular. And although the younger generation may not be indifferent to the hits of the West, there seems to be little distinction between 'pop' and folk-music.

All around the city is unspoiled country and there is no better way of enjoying it than to wander in the woods, or to follow the channels and sandbanks in a rowing-boat hired on the many lakes and rivers. Lake Mogoşoaia, some ten miles to the north-west, has an unequalled popularity on account of the famous palace built there in 1702 by Prince Constantin Brîncoveanu, now converted into the country's prime museum of Brancovan, and feudal art. Its graceful loggia whose arches are supported on twisted stone columns with florid capitals looks on to a garden filled with topiary and a lily pool. Its symmetry and some of its detail are almost Venetian, and the height of the roof is enhanced by two funnel-shaped chimneys suggesting the world of Alice in Wonderland. There are the remains of another Brancovan palace built in 1699 and re-nowned in its day, at Potlogi, not far from the main road to Piteşti. Its stucco designs reflect Persian influence. Directly north of Bucharest and sixteen miles beyond Băneasa is the Lake of Snagov, a favourite bathing resort with boating and camping where at week-ends half of Bucharest takes to the open air. There are excursions to Pustuicul and Cernica, wonderful stretches of woodland to the south of the city, and the latter distinguished by a fine monastery. At Giurgiu, an industrial river-port where a great bridge crosses the Dan-ube and its adjoining marshes to the Bulgarian city of Ruse, it is possible to take steamers such as the S.S. *Olteniţa* and S.S. *Carpaţi* to the lower Danube or as far as Budapest and Vienna. Near Vlăsia, at Căldărusani the site of another monastery, there is a lake for fishing and a beautiful forest in which game is hunted.

Roads and railways radiate in all directions from Bucharest and two of the most travelled head north to the oil city of Ploieşti and north-west to the industrial town of Piteşti whose new Renault factory will be producing 50,000 cars by 1970.

Despite the extraordinary industrial development of these areas, the upper Cîmpia (cîmpia is the Latin 'campo') and the undulating foothills of the Carpathians are largely culti- vated or else still thickly forested with oaks and beech-trees. This heartland of the old Wallachia, where farmland, vine- yards and rich orchards repose in hollow valleys, is as alive today as it was in the days when Cîmpulung, Curtea de Argeş and Tîrgovişte held sway over the whole of the prin- cipality.

Ploieşti, a large city whose destiny was determined by the striking of oil more than a century ago, positively glows at night, with its derricks ranged like titanic Christmas trees across the sky. Giant refineries, processing most of the coun- try's crude oil, tower above the fields and forest, their silver chimneys emitting sky-searing shots of flame. Though having a venerable history, Ploieşti rebuilt itself almost entirely after the air bombardments of the Second World War. Its monu- ments include a Republican Oil Museum (in the Strada Diligenţei) whose like cannot be seen this side of Texas, and the Caragiale Museum which is devoted to the life and work of the great Romanian dramatist who died in 1912. On the flanks of the Teleajen Valley, north of Ploieşti, is the resort of Vălenii de Munte, famous for its ţuica (plum brandy).

Further up is Slănic, a tourist centre and health resort, as well as one of the most important salt mines in Romania. The fame of the town is linked to the existence of a huge salt mas- sif in its subsoil. This massif rises west of the town in the form of a miniature mountain known as the Murtele de Sare (Salt Mountain), a wonderful natural monument whose iridescent colours sparkle in the sun. Salt began to be mined at Slănic in the second half of the 17th century, in the reign of Serban Cantacuzino, at a place known today under the name of Baia Verde. After landslides made the roads leading to the salt mines impassable, another mine was dug early in the second half of the 18th century at Baia Baciului, where the

salt mountain stands today. Although the salt is near the surface, the salt mountain, Slănic's present day point of attraction, was not visible at that time. According to the records,
two mine pits seem to have been dug at the time, one in the
then invisible salt mountain and one nearby, to the east.
The second shaft caved in and was filled with salt-water,
giving rise to Lake Baia Baciului. Massive landslides occurred,
then invisible salt mountain and one nearby, to the east. The
salt walls of the first mine were laid bare and the salt mountain appeared. Subject to dissolution, the layer covering the
mine vanished and a small extremely salted lake was formed
in the heart of the salt mountain, called Lac al Miresei (The
Bride's Lake). Legend has it that a bride forsaken on her
wedding day put an end to her troubles by casting herself
from a peak into the abyss below, at the bottom of which lies
the sparkling lake.

Rainwater has played a great part in moulding this extraordinary phenomenon; salt was dissolved to various extents
and the deep grooves that were formed revealed the strata of
the mountain. A gallery carved in the eastern wall of the old
salt mine at Baia Baciului leads to a deep pit. From this
gallery visitors can look down at the Bride's Lake with its
emerald green fringes. The middle of the lake reflects the
deep azure of the sky, seen through an opening above where
the roof of the mine caved in. The Bride's Lake is today a
national monument.

Near Cîmpina and off the main highway leading up the
Prahova Valley is the former prison of Doftana, now a
museum, in which political prisoners were detained and at
times subjected to inhuman treatment. Most of its cells possessed no windows and in the 1940 earthquake several of its
inmates died a grotesque death in the dark. The Prahova
Valley reaches to Sinaia and will be described in Chapter 6.

The horizon of Tîrgovişte is a motley of church-towers and
oil derricks, for this was Romania's oldest oil-producing
centre, but the outlying countryside still grows tobacco,

vines and fruit in abundance and Tîrgovişte itself, for all its building activity, boasts several superb examples of Wallachian art. The late 15th-century Dealul Monastery to which Michael the Brave's head was returned after his murder in Transylvania in 1601, has a 16th-century church of outstanding grace, with tall octagonal towers and the most intricate honeycombing of geometric stucco adorning its upper storeys. The ruins of the Princely Court which thrived so long as Tîgovişte was capital of Wallachia, are extant, but much more exciting is the 16th-century Prince's Church, a consummate work of symmetry and elegant, understated ornamentation. Its polychrome frescoes are in good shape and invite comparison with the best examples of Moldavian paintings; their brilliant use of gold enhances the lightness and warmth of the interior. On the north-western side of the palace is the Watchtower of Chindia, probably raised by Mircea the Old in the 15th century, an Italiante redoubt with a bassive base which served as a look-out for imminent invasions. From its summit, reached by a wooden spiral staircase, the vestiges of the old walls and the moat into which the River Ialomiţa was diverted in times of danger can be easily discerned. The town's History Museum is a treasure house of archaeological finds, including the neolithic Gumelniţa statuette excavated in 1960, and of many medieval items such as the double-eagle device carved on the tombstone of Princess Bălaşa Cantacuzino (1711). Of the several other churches in Tîrgovişte the most unusual is the 17th-century Stelea Church, which mixes Wallachian characteristics (such as its overall plan and a system of two-tiered exterior niches) with Moldavian components: the towers on a star-shaped drum in turn resting on a square base, the sculpted stone mouldings and so forth.

Beneath the magnificent backdrop of the Făgăraş and Bucegi Massifs of the Carpathians is the old town of Cîmpulung, developed before the 16th century as the first capital of Wallachia and a respectable city at that. The legendary 13th-century founder of Wallachia, Prince Radu Negru, is said to have built the original but since-restored Monastery of Negru Vodă which you see to this day. The town's history is traced in the local museum (Strada Republicii) and in the Prince's House, constructed in the 17th century by Prince Matei Basarab. A feature uncommon in the southerly parts of Wallachia but frequent in the marcher country of Transylvania where, of course, Catholic influences filtered through from the Magyars and Germans, is the 14th-century Gothic church of Bărăţia, quite distinctive in its context. And from Cîmpulung there are many agreeable walks in the forested foothills of the Carpathians, and from Voina-Păpuşa, eleven miles to the north, the Iezar-Păpuşa Range (8,000 feet) can be assailed, by a series of relatively simple and well-marked footpaths.

The third medieval town of old Wallachia, and the principality's second capital, is Curtea de Argeş, meaning Court of Argeş, well to the west of Cîmpulung, or, coming from Bucharest, to the north of Piteşti. Two of the oldest buildings in Wallachia are the Prince's Church, built in about 1330 and located among the ruins of the Prince's Court, and the 14th-century Church of St. Nicoara, both of which follow a standard Byzantine plan but possess a stylistic resemblance to the churches of Trnovo, the medieval capital of Bulgaria.

Most impressive at Curtea de Argeş is the famed Episcopal Church, built in the early 16th century by Prince Neagoe Basarab and restored eighty years ago by the French architect Lecomte du Nouy. It is set in a charming park and its exterior is encrusted with a wealth of carved stone mouldings evocative of Georgia and Armenia. Near the Episcopal Church there is a fountain whose provenance seems somewhat fanciful. A certain master-mason called Manole who had already buried his wife alive in the foundations of the church came to the end of his labours; no sooner had he dropped his tools and stood to admire the results from the church's roof than the patron Prince stepped up and pushed the luckless mason to the ground – to ensure that so skilled a man would never again build the likes of such a church. Where Manole fell, it is said, a fountain springs.

Till now few foreigners have ventured to these medieval capitals, a pity since, if time has not stood still, Tirgoviște, Cîmpulung and Curtea de Argeş reach back to the past more consistently than does Bucharest.

From the Middle Ages to modern technology is but fifteen miles of mountain road. Near Corbeni they are building a hydro-electric station with a massive arched dam across the narrow defile of the Argeş and soon a new lake will form in the amphitheatre of Romania's highest mountain.

To the north of the Carpathians lies Transylvania, to the east Moldavia, and to the west of the River Olt stretches Oltenia. We shall come to them in due course.

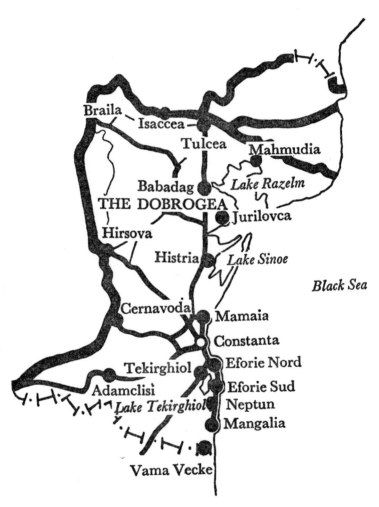

Braila
Isaccea
Tulcea
Mahmudia
Babadag *Lake Razelm*
THE DOBROGEA
Jurilovca
Hirsova
Histria *Lake Sinoe*

Black Sea

Cernavoda
Mamaia
Constanta
Eforie Nord
Tekirghiol
Adamclisi
Lake Tekirghiol
Eforie Sud
Neptun
Mangalia

Vama Vecke

CHAPTER THREE

The Dobrogea

*Bărăgan Plain – Bridge at Cernavodă – History, geography and
topography – Constanţa (Tomis) – Black Sea Coast resorts:
Mamaia, Eforie Nord and Eforie Sud, Neptun, Mangalia
(Callatis) – Ancient monuments and classical history of Dobrogea:
Adamclisi (Tropaeum Trajahi), Histria, Lake Razelm –
Archaeological discoveries – Danube Delta and its flora and fauna.*

Every afternoon the sleek express train from Bucharest to
Constanţa streaks like green lightning across the Bărăgan
Plain slowing only as it rumbles over the famous iron bridge
at Cernavodă. A highway also connects the capital with the
Black Sea coast by way of the ferry at Giurgeni, following a
less direct route than the train but suitable for those who have
the time to call at the spa of Amara on its salty and radioactive lake. This is the flattest land in Romania and the most
exposed to the elements. In winter the rich black earth wears
a blanket of snow but in spring is transformed into a green
sea of wheat and, a little later, maize. The harvesting of this
golden granary begins in June, considerably earlier than in
the northern parts of the country. The flatness of the landscape is in summer relieved by the dusty pattern of cart-
tracks and modern roadways cutting sharply through small
villages and straggling woodlands.

Before reaching Cernavodă the railway is carried high
across the two arms of the Danube on a bridge built in 1895
by Saligny, the brilliant Romanian engineer who, on the
opening day, stood in the shadow of his masterpiece in order

to prove its worth to the sceptics. This, the longest bridge in Europe at the time, more than anything else served to open up the region east of the Danube known as the Dobrogea after long centuries of dereliction. Ever since the Romans in A.D. 103 threw the first bridge across the upper reaches at Drubeta (modern Turnu-Severin), the Danube has posed great problems for the engineer and its lower reaches are even today spanned at only a few points. At Giurgeni a projected road bridge should replace, by the end of 1969, the ferries which at present transport cars and buses to the Dobrogea side at Hîrşova.

The Dobrogea is both the oldest and newest region of the country. When in classical times, as a southern extension of the Scythian Steppe, it was called Scythia Minor, its cities – Histria, Tomis, Callatis, Tropaeum Trajani – grew and prospered as ports, as centres of trade and culture and as settlements for a variety of peoples, but then despite Genoese attempts to restore it to its former eminence, the Dobrogea fell into a long decline virtually lasting the whole of the feudal and Turkish periods, and it was only when incorporated into the new state of Romania in 1878 and especially when Saligny built his bridge two decades later that the Dobrogea began once again to participate in the life of the nation. The human landmarks of the province consequently comprise on the one hand splendid ruins from a Graeco-Roman past and, on the other, the shining new hotels and villas of resort-towns that are springing up on the shores of the Black Sea. Elsewhere the countryside is relatively unpopulated; the torrential rains wash away so much of the top-soil that the rock is always close to the surface of the land. Natural vegetation means little more than stunted oaks, dry grass and a scattering of thistle and vetch; the rivers of the Dobrogea are short and unimportant but a chain of lagoon-and-bar formations follow the upper coast so that several large lakes, some of them saline, give the coast a scenic variety as well as an extraordinary range of wild life. In the north-east, the Delta of the Danube

5. The Sports Hotel at Poiana Braşov.

7. Landscape in the Apuseni Mountains.

6. *left:* The Village Museum in Bucharest.

8. The Sucevita Monastery in Northern Moldavia.

forms one of the most remarkable natural phenomena in the world, a vast labyrinth of river-channels on whose reedy banks is the large refuge of wild life in Europe, as yet free from human encroachment.

The Turks left here little but names such as Babadag, Mahmudia, Siutghiol and Tekirghiol, and the emptiness of the inland plain and plateaux, but do not suppose that the Dobrogea is, if it has been, the poor relation of the Romanian family. Arrive at its capital city of Constanţa and you will find a boom town that is simultaneously the country's largest port and the central link in a chain of burgeoning tourist resorts strung along the coast. In the post-war years the government has invested heavily in the future of all the Dobrogea and the crane and cement-mixer are a common denominator of Constanţa and the resorts alike. Constanţa was Tomis to the Romans and its name in legend derived from the Greek word 'tomi' (meaning 'piece') to commemorate the bloody fate of Abysyrtus, the little son of King Aetes of Colchis, who during the voyage of the Argonauts was dismembered piece by piece by his fugitive sister Medea off the shores of the future city. In fact, like Histria founded a century earlier, Tomis was colonised by Greeks from Miletus in the 6th century B.C. and it gradually supplanted Histria as the chief city of Western Pontus. It was to thrive and expand under Roman administration and in the 4th century A.D., when close links with Byzantium were maintained, Tomis was renamed Constantiana in honour of the Emperor Constantine's sister. In the late 6th century the city entered the winter of its long decay; the Avars razed much of it and the subsequent (13th century) interest of Genoese merchants in restoring the great harbour brought it only short-lived benefits. Most of the city belongs then, to our century and, apart from the vestiges of the ancient port, there is not too much *in situ* to recall the grandeur of the past. An open-air museum in the Bulevard Republicii reveals sections of the Roman Wall and a Byzantine tower but only the most recent discoveries are yielding items that are both aesthetically and historically significant. One of these is the magnificent mosaic excavated in 1959 near the County Council Building, now fully cleared for public inspection. Its multicoloured geometric and floral pattern covers a large area and appears to have been the floor of a Byzatine emporium.

In the Piaţa Independenţei there is a bronze statue done in 1887 by Ferrari in honour of Ovid who, much against his will, was exiled to this part of Pontus in 9 A.D. by the Emperor Augustus and who died at Tomis seven years later. Here the poet composed his 'Tristia' and 'Pontica', revised the 'Metamorphoses' and finished the 'Fasti', from his own accounts esteemed and honoured by the local citizenry. His name lives in several institutions and in a township near Mamaia.

Tomis is very much alive, however, in the big collection at the Dobrogea Archaeological Museum in the Strada Muzeelor, containing as it does the ceramics, statues, base-reliefs and coins of several epochs. And what of the modern city? More than anywhere else in Romania, the fusion and juxtaposition of several styles is most evident in Constanţa. The The Casino (1904), now a restaurant, is a cosmopolitan and capricious memorial to the age of palm-court orchestras and bath-houses; nearby stand a large Aquarium and the restored Genoese lighthouse. A bust of Mihail Eminescu, Romania's greatest lyric poet (1850–1889) gazes out to the sea which inspired much of his writing. There are large Turkish, Greek, Tatar and other minorities who have made Constanţa their home for centuries. A Turkish mosque is in use every Friday, its minaret an excellent vantage point; a Spanish-speaking synagogue bears witness to the colony of Sephardic Jews who live in Romania, and the towers of the Greek Orthodox Church observe limits imposed in 1867 upon their architect by a Sultan who forbade the construction of any church that exceeded the height of the several mosques in town.

Constanţa is now transforming itself at a rapid pace; the straight and tree-lined avenues of the new city are dominated by rectangular residential blocks in the pastel shades so appropriate to sunny latitudes. A brand-new railway station and the extraordinary lighthouse, both built in 1960, are an exciting adventure in the geometry of reinforced concrete. Though our traveller is unlikely to exchange the sybaritical amenities of the coastal resorts for the more serious setting of a port and industrial city, he is well recommended a few hours of wandering in the narrow streets of the old town, especially in the evening when the little cafés are alive with music and multilingual gossip and when a cool breeze creeps up from the narrow promontory. Constanţa is also the communications hub of the Dobrogea; all the Romanian coastal resorts and classical sites are easily reached from here and there are land, sea and air excursions made to Bucharest, to the painted monasteries of Moldavia, to the Delta of the Danube, to the Bulgarian coast and even to Odessa, Istanbul Athens.

In Romania the tourist industry is currently evolving faster than anywhere in Europe and the Black Sea coast sets the pace for the rest of the country. For northern visitors there is firstly the sheer natural attractiveness of the beaches, lakes and lagoons and secondly the novelty of a region which has only recently featured in the travel supplements of Sunday newspapers. It is to be feared that some visitors who descend in charter-planes at Constanţa Airport from Manchester and Malmö, Dresden and Düsseldorf, are sun-worshippers content exclusively to absorb twelve hours of daily sunlight and warmth on the soft sandy shores of the Black Sea, to partake of the well-arranged night-life of the chief resorts and then to return home not only as the bronze idols of their own communities but as Romanian experts. Certainly the climatic incentives of the coast cannot be underestimated, but nor should the classical beauties of Histria and Adamclisi or the nature wonderland of the Delta be forgotten, for these are in themselves worth a trip all the way across Europe. A balanced diet of coast, historical sights and Delta is easily digestible and, indeed, is even spoon-fed to the less adventurous by the competent polyglot guides and interpreters who are stationed in the hotels, eating places and clubs of Mamaia, Eforie and Mangalia. After a morning pilgrimage to the Museum and mosaics of Constanţa it is perfectly simple to return to the solar ritual of the afternoon. This much said, what is special about the new resorts, apart from their striking modernity? Since they face east, their beaches and floral promenades and hotel windows watch the sun till it drops into the shimmering sea; the sand is so soft that it takes the imprint of the recumbent sunbather and the sea so shallow that the wader can feel the radiant warmth of the sand on his feet. For at least eight months of the year preponderant if not total sunshine is the order of the day. The curative properties of the salt, sulphur, radioactive and other springs found all over Romania have already been mentioned; for those who seek treatment such coastal spas as Eforie and Mangalia combine therapy with the pleasures of the seaside. And finally there is the undeniable convenience of townships organised with the vacationist in mind; Mamaia, for instance, exists solely for tourism and by tourism and in the short winter months it bolts its doors and shutters its windows.

Mamaia, four miles north of Constanţa, resembles Miami Beach in more than name. Like the sun-centre of the Florida seaboard it hugs a narrow isthmus between a lake and the open sea, has an eastward exposure, caters first and foremost to groups and families, adopts a contemporary if not futuristic style of building and is proving a trail-blazer in its own continent. But for all those affinities its name is Turkish; it is still quite small and is truly cosmopolitan, visited nonetheless by swarms of day-trippers from Constanţa and by holiday-makers from inland Romania. The secret of its mild summer climate lies in the fact that the fresh water of Lake Siutghiol which Mamaia straddles on the west creates sufficient evaporation to protect the town from the often excessive heat of the Dobrogea.

Of the pre-war Mamaia, little remains save the Baroque royal residence, an austere casino, several villas and some very fine vegetation. Mamaia is thus mainly a child of the 1950's and '60's; its forty gleaming glass hotels, reminiscent of Brasilia and modern Beirut, are imposing and anonymous. Adjacent to them are smaller structures set at less deliberate angles, all within a few bare footsteps from the broad flower-decked promenade and the beach. At the top of the shore wind-cheating shrubs enclose small bays of warmth for sun-bathing on stormier days; these seen to be inhabited by Germans in deckchairs. Kiosks sell chairs and parasols, real Pilsener beer and real Pepsi Cola. At night the boardwalks are hung with coloured lights, music from the discothéques and dance halls fills the air. At the Miorița there is the spirited folk music of traditional Romania and jolly 'evenings with Bacchus' are arranged in the country.

Eforie Nord and, three miles down, Eforie Sud, are resorts to the south of Constanța, whose character is altogether different from Mamaia's. Eforie Nord is the more appealing; the town, for all its wide boulevards and modern buildings, is perfectly integrated with its natural setting of gentle hills and tall, luxuriant foliage. Paths in the reddish cliffs give quick access to the sandy shore; an agreeable balance of shade and sunlight has been struck and even the glamorous and shapely Hotel Europa seems to retire behind its frond of pines, palms and cypresses. The two parts of Eforie are joined by a sandspit on whose leeward side lies Lake Tekirghiol, so salty that in legend it takes its name from Tekir, an unsuspecting Turkish horseman who vainly endeavoured to end his life by pluning in its muddy and unpredictably buoyant waters. The chemical content and tepid temperatures of this lake have given rise to several sanatoria and even an open-air mud bath on its banks.

Beyond Eforie a new holiday complex suggestively named

Neptun rises from the former marshes and scrub. Its spacious gardens slope down to the little bay and a jetty where yachts are moored. Buildings are attuned to the tastes of the late 1960's and their human scale makes for a sense of relaxation. The main hotel has a plastic beauty absent in the monumental blocks of the earlier Mamaia; the veranda at one end encloses an open patio where an ancient tree projects its sculptured branches to the sky. Each room has a balcony with a view of the sea or the game forest that stretches south towards Mangalia. The ample use of white walls, light wood and fibre-glass gives a totally pleasing effect of lightness and grace. As yet this tiny resort is hardly known and for that reason has a mirage-like quality.

The southernmost town on the Romanian coast is Mangalia, twenty-seven miles from Constanţa. Enjoying an exceptionally mild Mediterranean type of climate, Mangalia will by 1970 surpass Mamaia as the biggest of the coastal resorts. The low cliffs above the beach are already fringed with ultra-modern hotels and restaurants and there is a busy traffic of excursion trains, boats and buses converging here. The old Graeco-Roman walled city of Callatis, founded by Dorian colonists from Asia Minor and named after the River Calles which they left behind, is now almost entirely submerged under the modern town but recent excavations have unearthed many antiquities, some of which are exhibited in the Mangalia Museum.

The Black Sea coast of Romania, as of Bulgaria, is becoming an international playground; each winter the surveyors and bulldozers stretch the limits of the existing resorts and found new holiday centres in the marshes and dunes. From being Romania's poorest region, the Dobrogea, in a matter of one decade, is turning into one of the richest provinces under the sun.

Before proceeding to the Delta it is as well to consider the ancient monuments of the Dobrogea, divided fairly equally between the museums of Constanţa and Mangalia and the handful of sites already excavated. Full credit must be given to the work of the National Museum of Antiquities and the Archaeological Institute in Bucharest which, since 1948, has led to the most exciting discoveries of prehistoric and classical remains, not only in Dobrogea (ancient Scythia Minor) but also in historic Dacia, which is modern Oltenia and Transylvania. The ample volumes of 'Dacia-Journal of Archaeology and Ancient History' testify, in five languages including English, to their massive achievements. The first inhabitants who lived on the territory of present-day Romania were the Geto-Decians, a branch of the Thracians but, beginning with the 7th century B.C. several Greek slave-owning colonies were established on the Dobrogean shore of the Black Sea, such as Histria, Callatis and Tomis, which retained close links with the native population. The Kings of the Getae were for centuries the protectors of those cities. The Dacian tribal unions merged in the 1st century B.C. to form the Dacians' first state under Burebista, which was to reach its zenith under Decebal (A.D. 87–106). Archaeological diggings made in recent years, especially on the site of Sarmizegetusa, the Dacian capital, have brought to light rich material indicating a high and original civilisation.

Following two fierce wars (101–102 and 105–106) Dacia was conquered by the Romans under Trajan and was to remain a province of the Empire till the year 271. In this latter period the Black Sea coast was linked to the rest of the Empire not only by the Danube and a long sea route but also by a road which entered Dacia to the west by way of the famous Iron Gates. This was the great marching route of the legionaries and it also strung together the Dacian cities which the Romans transformed with the civic monuments, fortifications, villas and baths. In Dacia proper, the chief Roman cities were Sarmizegetusa, Drubeta and Apulum (Alba Iulia); in the Dobrogea and Wallachia (which the Latins called Moesia), Histria, Tropaeum Trajani (modern Adamclisi) and Callatis were the principal centres. To this day these places represent several cultural layers but at Histria, for example, the vestiges of the Graeco-Roman presence are particularly evident, side by side with native Geto-Dacian and later Byzantine remains. The Roman legacy survives in more than the mere name of the Romanian state. The language of Romania is fundamentally a variant of Latin with many borrowings from Slav and other sources; the Romanian notions of law (Romanian 'lege'), sin ('pacat') and duty ('datoria') may in part be traced to the Roman experience. Most of all the people of Romania consciously foster a Latin tradition even though they are aware that many of their customs and art forms such as the famous national dance, the 'hora', may go back to Thracian beginnings. And a nation is, ultimately, what it believes itself to be.

From Constanța, as we have seen, journeys to the outlying areas of the Dobrogea are simply undertaken. One of these, by road, veers forty miles south-west to Adamclisi. On the way, at Murfatlar, there are renowned vineyards set in the hot limestone hills and producing sweet and fragrant wines, both red and white. The village commune maintains a viticultural research station at Murfatlar and it is quite possible to inspect the vineyards and later taste their velvety wines in the cellars. The highway continues across a high plain to the early 2nd-century A.D. ruins of Tropaeum Trajani, or Trajan's Trophy, on a plateau above the modern village of Adamclisi. This city was built by the Romans to commemorate their victory over the Dacians in a battle in which the Emperor Trajan himself may have fought. Its most interesting features are the forty-nine limestone metopes that decorated the original cylindrical plinth. These depict in lucid detail scenes and personalities of the campaign: Trajan inspecting his troops, a chariot fight, two captives led before the Emperor. There are also some fine and telling fragments of friezes, sculptures and inscriptions. Below the plateau, in a broad valley, is a Roman fortress erected by Trajan, one of the best preserved in Eastern Europe. The remnants of solid outer walls with their wide entrance gates, a main street and extensive ruins of basilicas with the bases of their columns still intact give a good idea of the original configuration.

On the road and not far from the railway between Constanța and the Delta town of Tulcea stands the magnificent site of Histria, probably the most memorable classical monument and certainly the oldest in Romania. Set in a barren landscape of sun-blenched grass and ochre vegetation, the white mass of its fortifications can be descried from afar.

The three walls of Histria, one Greek and two Roman, are in a relatively good condition and their summit affords a fine view over the ancient city and Lake Sinoe. Inside the fortress the marble paving-stones are deeply rutted by the wheels of the Roman chariots which passed in and out through a gate guarded by tall turrets. Most striking are the ruins of several establishments of the imperial cults and of culture, among which the temple of Aphrodite and the temple of Zeus, with Ionic columns still standing from the Greek period, a Roman forum, thermae, mosaics, marble sculptures, pottery and inscriptions. Some of Histria's very finest archaic ceramics, chiefly of Corinthian and Rhodian provenance, can be seen at the Museum in Constanța. Histria was founded in 600 B.C., on what then formed the seashore, by Greeks from Miletus as a trading centre. It remained the chief city in Western Pontus until eclipsed by Tomis and Callatis, and it maintained constant commercial contacts with Rhodes, Miletus, Athens and Corinth. By the 2nd century B.C., however, internal unrest and the silting up of the harbour reduced its importance and together with the other cities of the Hellenic coastal strip, it entered into an alliance with King Mithridates VI on Pontus. During the subsequent Roman era, Histria thrived under imperial protection. A splendid plumbing system was devised whereby water was carried in aqueducts from twenty miles away. In 248 the city fell to the

Gothic barbarians and was razed, but its citizens lovingly re-built it, adding some of those touches of luxury which we know from Pompeii and also a high wall for protection. Under the renewed Roman aegis Histria thrived again till, by the 7th century, with some unknown disaster, it ceased to be. Its harbour stagnated, its buildings became derelict and overgrown with weeds and its population dispersed. Not until 1914 was Histria re-discovered, by the Romanian archae-ologist Vasile Pârvan.

The journey north from Histria continues over a dry plain bordering Lakes Sinoe and Razelm and relieved occasionally by slight uplands covered with vineyards, meadows and low forest. Just off the road is Hamangia, site of a recently exca-vated neolithic culture, now celebrated for its striped ceram-ics and its female figurines suggestive of a fertility cult and bearing definite affinities with the contemporaneous arts of Troy and the Cyclades. It is appropriate to mention here that a number of recent excavations throughout the Balkans and South-East Europe but notably in Romania, Yugoslavia and Greece, point to outstanding neolithic cultures existing in the area from 5,000 B.C. onwards and indicate societies that could have rivalled those of Egypt, Iran, Mesopotamia and Asia Minor and, in certain cases, may have predated *all* the known cultures of the Near East. According to the ceramic finds of the Austrian archaeologist Schachermeyr made be-fore 1954, the oldest of these Balkan phenomena was the Starčevo culture of the fifth millenium B.C., located in the vicinity of modern Belgrade. Up until 1956 the first known neolithic culture in Romania was believed to be that of the Criş civilisation, represented by sites in Moldavia (Glăvăn-eştii Vechi) and Transylvania (Leţ) dating from 4,200 B.C. but diggings accomplished in the Ceahlau Mountains of Moldavia in the last decade have brought forth pottery con-siderably older.

Sixty miles north of Constanţa on a branch road leading from Babadag you can see the relics of Roman Heracleia on a prospect above the village of Eni ala. And to the south, on Lake Razelm, is the attractive fishing settlement of Jurilovca, famous throughout Romania for its excellent, if expensive, caviar. Lake Razelm now seethes with fish but at one time there were important human colonies along its shore. The remains of the Byzantine city of Dolo man, perched on a tall rock above the lake, guard the whole region. On an island at the mouth of the lake, the ruins of another Byzantine fort still stand; these are not so easily reached by public transport but are worth exploring. The entire northern Dobrogea is, indeed, peppered with Byzantine and Roman sites – at Salsovia in the Delta, at Igli a, Isaccea and Hîr ova and about halfway between the Danube and the sea, there is the Roman fortress of Ulmetum. At Capidava, near Cernavod , the walls of a Romano-Byzantine castle dominate the Danube from a bluff.

The Danube Delta lies at the end of the long road from the tourist coast, but it is easily accessible by the air, train, boat and road services operating from several points in Romania and converging at the gateway town of Tulcea. From here the Danube branches out into three main channels, Chilia, Sulina and Sf. Gheorghe, through which it carries its water to the sea. Quite unlike anything else, the Delta, continually shifting and changing, is one of the few natural environments in Europe. This gigantic and incessant transformation of the Delta has been proceeding for centuries. 'By dividing and spreading itself across the Delta', noted the Romanian writer Vlahu , 'it seems as if the Danube were trying to hide and flee the irresistible attraction of the sea, whose waves call from afar...'

The Danube Delta was already mentioned in antiquity. According to an Egyptian legend, the god Osiris passed that way. It seems that the name of Istros, by which the Danube was called for a long time, dates from those days. Herodotus asserts that the Egyptian priests of Thebes possessed a book describing the expedition made by Pharoah Sesostris in the

Delta. Certainly Herodotus himself visited the Mouths of the Danube 2,400 years ago and his description shows that the Delta was then quite different from what it is today. Instead of marshes, forests of reeds, and sandbars, there was a huge estuary.

There was a time when the level of the Black Sea was much lower and the Delta was a wide plain through which the Danube flowed calmly towards the sea, its banks being then inhabited by monkeys and rhinoceroses. Several tributaries joined the river from north and south. Then came another period when the Sea was much higher than today and spread as far as Galați and Brăila and even to Giurgiu. But still today the Delta is in process of formation. The forces of nature which shape it, the struggle between land and water, the contrast between different environments, the mixture of animals typical of every kind of habitat give rise to phenomena which repeat in this immense 'laboratory of nature' the metamorphoses that took place throughout the depression of the Romanian Plain during the Quaternary period. 'The boundless expanse of water', wrote the late prosemaster Sadoveanu, 'covering a whole region, formed a realm of mystery. The boat slumbering among the reeds, the swans and pelicans whose wings ruffle the dark pools at night, the population of small birds, the teeming fish and the myriad unknown and unpredictable insects – all find nourishment in these waters which extend their rich empire and carry down the fertile silt from the distant mountains and plains. The strife to create life and the struggle for a ray of light and a scrap of food has been going on in the Delta for thousands of years, from the azure heights above down to the muddy depths. Endless generations have fallen. They have been turned into silt and fed the sources of new life.'

Formerly a gulf to which the Danube brought down more and more silt, the Danube Delta is one of the largest deltas in the world, surpassing the swamps known as Las Marismas at the mouth of the Spanish Guadalquivir and the Camargue

Delta of the Rhone in the variety and abundance of its wild life. Its mild climate, influenced by the Black Sea, the regular spring floods lasting for three or four months when the river rises by up to 15 feet, its isolation, all have helped the evolution of an infinite diversity of flora and fauna of unparalleled beauty; this beauty is the more striking since man's activity has tamed other similar environments.

In late spring the Delta is freshest; willows sweeten the air and nightingales and larks accompany the waterbound traveller on perpetually blue waves. Then in summer it resembles a limitless green forest of reeds, one of these varieties even attaining a height of 14 feet. This verdant sea is interrupted by countless pools and dry sandbanks called *grinduri*. A compact layer of rhyzomes and fibrous roots has formed under this green forest beginning at the edge of the pools and advancing towards the middle of the water. It grows thicker every year owing to plant humus, animal deposits and the silt brought down by floods. They layer floats on the surface of the water, lifting with the floods and dropping with the level of the water. A rich fauna, mainly birds and a few animals, inhabit these floating islands, which can be reached when the water is low. It is, moreover, along the waterways and channels which run between the floating islands, linking the pools and the villages, that all traffic in the Delta moves. The sediments deposited by floods form banks, the higher part being protected from the sea, some covered with white willows or with black poplars yielding ten times as much timber as conifers in the mountain areas, other converted into fields and pasture.

The lush vegetation of the Delta is extremely varied. Floating plants such as white and yellow water-lilies and crowfoot and the extraordinary 'water-nuts' with their rhomboid leaves carpet the surface of the pools and a whole world of amphibian plants develops in the undergrowth. The steppe meadows on the sandbanks are, until June when most of the species dry in the warm sea wind, ablaze with the silvery leaves of the creeping willow and flowering milkweed.

The Delta's attraction as a veritable paradise of birds, especially in spring and autumn when five of the most important bird migrations pass over it, is already well known to the ornithologist. No one, however, can fail to be impressed by the sheer range of living creatures; nightingales, egrets, spoonbills, cormorants, great northern and snow geese, northern duck, eagles and ospreys of many types inhabit the Delta in different seasons and on the eastern bank of the Chilia channel there is a reservation where nests the only big pelican colony in Europe. The sight of the young pelican feeding from the parent gullet is unforgettable, the father or mother pelican removing the whole skeleton of the fish from the beak of its offspring. In the marshes near the coast you will see the nesting grounds of mute swans which, in solitary pairs, go off and build their nests at a great distance from one another. In the autumn thousands of cranes, arriving from the cornfields of the Dobrogea, spend the night in the swamps while whole flocks of swans, geese and duck make the sandspit their winter headquarters.

There are animals too: mink, otter, ermine, foxes, wild cats, muskrat and even wolves. Large herds of wild boar live on the numerous islands of floating reed. Lizards and tortoises inhabit the sandbanks. The Delta boasts almost one hundred species of fish, the most interesting of which are the sturgeon, from which black caviar is obtained. Some sturgeon come from the sea to lay their eggs in the Danube, whilst others never leave the river.

Reed harvesting begins in November, when birds have returned to their winter dwellings; floating harvesters are used to reap this brittle forest, its cellulose destined for a variety of uses such as fine fabrics and the cording of car tyres. In the late winter large stretches of reed are burned in order to extend the harvesting areas.

To scientists and ordinary nature-lovers alike the Delta presents a most unusual spectacle. 'Can there be a people in this world that did not halt on the banks of the Danube?' wondered Sadoveanu. 'All the different languages of this Earth, the tumult, the clamours for life, the howls of eternal damnation have echoed here without disturbing the ever-lasting aspect of its marshes, except when a ripple spreads stirring the reeds.'

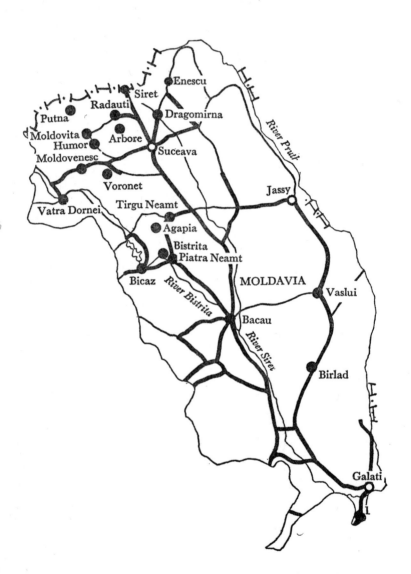

CHAPTER FOUR

Moldavia

*History – Suceava – Rural Moldavia – Painted churches and
monasteries: their techniques, aesthetics and history; Humor,
Moldoviţa, Arbore, Voroneţ, Suceviţa – Marginea ceramics –
country wedding – Putna monastery – Rădăuţi, capital of
Southern Bucovina – Dragomirna monastery – George Enescu, his
life and work – Spas of Cîmpulung Moldovenesc and Vatra Dornei –
natural wonders of Pietrele Doamnei – Lake Bicaz – Bicaz Gorges –
Lacul Roşu – Neamţ monastery – Jassy (Iaşi) – Port cities of
Galaţi and Brăila.*

In the museum of the Putna Monastery on the northern
frontier of Moldavia you will see a map of all the territories
held by one of the greatest heroes of Romanian history, Stephen the Great, 15th century Prince of Moldavia. Since the
boundaries of the Moldavian principality met those of
several expansionist neighbours, Poles, Magyars, Tatars and
Turks, Stephen – called by Pope Pius VI the 'athlete of
Christ' in recognition of his services to the Christian West –
built a ring of splendid fortifications, from Hotin and Suceava
in the north to the Danubian town of Galaţi in the far south,
turning his country into a forward defence against the Turk.
In the words of the Romanian historian Nicolae Iorga, the
Turks in Moldavia fought against walls of granite. Behind
these sturdy defences there developed one of the most remarkable cultures in Europe: churches and palaces, en-
closed by high walls, towers and galleries, rose from hilltops
and from the hollows of secluded wooded valleys. The efflore-

65

scence of a culture cannot take place without the prior existence of a fertile imagination and a spirit of resolution. These
qualities found their complete expression in Stephen and in
his son Petru Rareş. Their finest monuments, the churches
and monasteries of northern Moldavia, have miraculously
survived till our time as a crystallisation of the principality's
golden age, which lasted till the Turks defeated Petru Rareş
in 1538. But Moldavia is not merely a living museum of the
Middle Ages. The multi-faceted city of Jassy or the ebullient
river ports of Galaţi and Brăila seem to train their eyes on the
future rather than the past. This juxtaposition of old and new
which all over Romania is so striking, is no less evident in
Moldavia than elsewhere.

It is quite possible to jump on a small TAROM plane at
Constanţa when an early morning Black Sea mist covers the
tarmac, and to fly north over a landscape of tawny hills
threaded with the silvery weave of numerous rivers and, one
hour later, to circle over a smiling countryside into which a
prospect of domes, spires, towers and chimneys gradually
swims. This is Suceava, the early capital of Moldavia (till
1565), today the rapidly growing centre of its region, with a
huge new hospital, tall housing blocks and the installations of
an important timber and paper industry. Situated on a pine-
covered slope above rich farmland and surrounded by higher
hills, it is a pleasant place, especially on a Sunday when the
peasants from miles around come to town dressed in their
brilliant and immaculate folk costume. Suceava's oldest
monument is the late 14th-century citadel, much restored,
with a fine moat and drawbridge, considerable vestiges of its
walls and a good view across to the old town. Suceava flou-
rished under Stephen the Great when trading links with all
corners of Europe and the Near East converged here and
helped finance the building of churches and other symbols of
new found greatness. The Church of the Monastery of St.
George, with its tall towers, its glazed roof of coloured tiles,
its fine painted interior now darkened by age and smoke,

gives some idea of Suceava's former wealth. Attacked and ravaged several times by Turks, Poles and Magyars, the city rose every time from its ashes. In 1538 Suliman the Magnificent and then again in 1624 the Tatars burned so much of it that only the outer walls and a few churches survived.

Suceava is situated in one of the loveliest stretches of country imaginable, where villages, mixed forest and pasture harmonise in a scene of near perfection. The roads are quite uncluttered and you can travel many miles withou seeing a motor vehicle – only a huddle of peasants enjoying a smoke, the kerchiefed heads of women working in the fields or an ox-drawn cart on its way to market. In the villages there is nothing to disturb an almost timeless tranquillity save the rumble of wooden carts, the cackle of stray geese and the chatter of villagers. The peasant house is cool, neat and substantial, nearly always embroidered with floral and abstract stucco designs in green, white or yellow, or else white-wahed to deflect the sunlight. Vines and vegetables hang from its eaves and, often enough, a wooden gateway twice or thrice a man's size and carved with intricate patterns, separates it from the road.

From Suceava you can travel easily to the painted churches and monasteries but it would be a big mistake to try to see more than two or three in one day, for each is a little world unto itself; its architecture, extraordinary mural painting, and the beauty of its setting demand as much time as you can give. These churches, erected by the feudal princes in the 15th and 16th centuries, were built in a style in which elements of Byzantine and Gothic inspiration were creatively adapted to local use. The most characteristic feature of Moldavian art is the exterior painting: the outside walls of the churches are literally covered from ground to roof with biblical and historical pictures, of saints, procession and epic happenings, which to this day have preserved their warm and brilliant hues. Of the fourteen extant churches with external frescoes, five are particularly notable, those at Humor (done in 1535),

Moldoviţa (1537), Arbore (1541), Voroneţ (1547) and Suceviţa (*c.* 1600). Closely related in style they were modelled on one another and together they probably represent the apogee of medieval art in Romania.

That entire surfaces of a church, both inside and out should be painted is rare, but not unknown elsewhere: in Catalonia, Russia and Armenia, for instance. What makes these Moldavian buildings so exceptional is their quality, their remarkable resilience over the centuries and the central rôle which they play in the national culture of Romania. Moldavian winters are notoriously cruel but only the north or north-easterly walls of the painted churches have suffered the erosion and effacement of blizzard winds from Siberia. No one is certain of the techniques used by the anonymous painters of four centuries ago, but it is likely that a plaster base containing sand and lime was first applied, followed by the actual process of painting. The palette from which so many durable colours derived probably consisted of red (from madder), yellow (from ochre or unripened ears of wheat), black (from soot and charcoal), blue (from the indigo plant or lapis lazuli) and gold. Each of these paints was strengthened and fluidised by an admixture of cow's bile and egg-yolk, both of which are resistant to weather.

The impact of Byzantine art, so strong in Greece, Serbia and Bulgaria, had already in the 14th century been felt in the Bogdan Church at nearby Rădăuţi and in the Cozia Monastery of Oltenia, and elsewhere too in Romania. What is so striking about the painted churches of Moldavia is that they post-date by at least fifty years the fall of Constantinople to the Ottoman Turks. As a modern historian has put it, Moldavian art is a posthumous child of Byzantine art. There are as a result many frescoes documenting, in none too flattering a light, the sieges and victories of the Turks, yet true to the main traditions of Byzantine painting.

It is worth remembering that the painted churches were not imperial monuments but simply the focal points of a village or monastery. Their spectacular frescoes served to educate and arouse a peasantry that neither was allowed into church nor knew how to read the scriptures, nor understood the Slavonic liturgy. But while the anonymous artists knew their biblical history rather well, at the same time they proved to be most inventive, and the fantastic portrayal of Gehenna or of human beings disgorged by carnivous beasts invite a comparison with the grotesqueries of Gothic sculpture or the monstrous pictorial feasts of Hieronymous Bosch.

The first of the most important churches is that at the monastery of Humor, lying in a shallow valley to the west of Suceava. Without a tower and with the basic 'three-cusp' plan of naos (or nave) and apses, it is one of the simplest churches in design, its surface being relieved only by the plasters imposed on the side apses and a clerestory motif below the high-pitched roof. Its west front, shielded by an open portico rather than by the usual closed narthex, displays a fiery Last Judgement and on the south wall the stirring story of how Constantinople was saved from the Persians in 626 is re-enacted in vivid colours, with the Persians suggestively dressed as Turks. The interior, with its dark ultramarine walls emblazoned with gold contains a richly carved wooden iconostasis and six 15th-century icons brought from an earlier church.

Up the river from Humor, standing in a steep, almost Alpine, valley is the fortress-monastery of Moldoviţa built by the voivod Petru Rareş on the site of an earlier monastery destroyed by an avalanche. Its outer walls are nearly 20 feet high and the church's exterior frescoes are exceptional, even by local standards. On the south wall against a blue background, an imaginative Tree of Jesse, including not only the biblical prophets but also such classical philosophers as Aristotle, traces the ancestry of Christ. Also on the south façade is another realistic representation of the 7th-century Persian siege. The Persians, again attired in Turkish clothing, are shown floundering in a confusion of gigantic waves, capsizing ships and sinking cannon while the Patriarch, Emperor and Empress of Byzantium, under a banner of the Virgin, command the defence of the city from its tall and grey symmetrical ramparts. In this representation the weaponry is contemporary and Constantinople resembles the Moldavian citadel of Neamț.

One wonders at the propagandistic effects of these pictorial pageants upon the mass of people who would gather outside at the end of a service. Remembering that the rank and file could not go beyond the pronaos and that even the landowners never penetrated the inner sanctuary where the most valuable icons were placed, the moral and political impact of such realistic murals on the exterior walls must have been the 16th century equivalent of the modern cinema and press. Unlike so many static Russian icons or, for that matter the pious art of the West, their vital and dynamic narrative quality can only have fortified the peasantry's faith in their creed and country and sharpened their hostility towards the Turk. This great creative epoch coincided, after all, with the Ottoman conquest of Modavia yet, within canonical limits, the incarnation of evil in these pictures often took a Turkish form and, ironically, the Turks – who spared few fortresses from demolition – left untouched these living symbols of spiritual resistance!

The church at Arbore resembles its neighbour Humor in its architectural simplicity, but that of Voroneț founded in 1488 by Stephen the Great, allegedly on the advice of a hermit, and set in Alpine meadows encircled by mountains and pinewoods, has some exceptional features, including a south façade whose frescoes, with their predominant indigo tones, run riot on the walls in the manner of a Tiepolo. The west front displays a superb Last Judgement in which Gehenna, the River of Fire, consumes naked sinners, in which angels run their spears through grisly black devils, shrouded dead rise from their graves and savage lions, bears and snakes regurgitate, limb by limb, the mortals on which they have recently feasted. 'So that all may be judged . . .' se ems to be the artist's message. Inside the church is a votive picture of Stephen the Great, the best portrayal of him in existence. The strong face, framed between chestnut curls, sharp features and robust shoulders, suggest the legendary determination and energy of this great prince.

Finally there is the great monastery of Suceviţa entrenched behind massive walls in a sunlight fold of wooded hills. This, the last of the churches with exterior frescoes, was built in 1584 by the Movilă family and painted in 1602–1604. It is excellently preserved and, with its massive ramparts and turrets, would make an ideal film set for Hollywood spectaculars. The north wall of the church is covered with a composition showing the Ladder of Heaven, each rung of which marks a mortal sin. For every transgression there is a macabre demon with wings and horns ready to drag the luckless sinner to hell. Just before vespers at Suceviţa a round-faced nun makes a full circle around the church, tapping the walls and beating a gong whose resonance echoes in the hills. Meanwhile, inside, six or seven nuns take turns to intone the litany; the hypnotic spell of its repetitive and other-wordly chant, based upon strong folk idiom, is broken only by the dissonance of one jovial sister who happens to be stone-deaf. Several of these churches are monasteries, and, though attendance is seldom full, the services have lost none of their traditional dignity. The interior at Suceviţa is wonderful, with lavish paintings of the Last Supper and Pantocrator and processional groups.

Near Suceviţa is the village of Marginea whose wooden houses are typically adorned with carvings and stucco. This is the home of a ceramics industry dating from Celtic times and it is well worth inspecting – and buying – some of its black pottery. The colour is obtained by smoking and polishing the pot before the clay has hardened.

If you are fortunate, which may be the case at week-ends, you will witness a wedding in one of the local hamlets or villages. The Moldavian country marriage is celebrated by all the community. Villagers young and old dress up in their elaborate rural finery, men in white tunics and black boots and women in richly embroidered blouses and red skirts; the children ride in haycarts drawn by horses decked with flowers and ribbons while the bridal couple, attired like the rest, are serenaded by an accordion band. The unbidden stranger is made welcome and the whole company is evidently very happy to be photographed. As yet, one feels, the encounter with a tourist is as rare to the Moldavian countryside as is the sight of so pastoral a wedding to the tourist.

So much for the painted churches, but there are several others without external frescoes that are exceptional in their own right, and easily accessible moreover. At Putna, not far to the north of Sucevița, is a sober stone monastery which one poet has called the 'temple of the national conscience'. Originally conceived in 1481 as a royal residence, it possesses certain Gothic features and is revered as the final resting place of Stephen the Great. Its museum contains manuscripts, icons and embroidery. There is at Putna a hotel in the style of a hunting-lodge where the visitor can recharge his energies for the next day. He should rise at dawn and climb the hillock behind – and be rewarded with a panorama, and atmosphere, of infinite calm.

Then, at the old town of Rădăuți on the road back to Suceava you can visit the little whitewashed church of Bogdan, the oldest building in Moldavia, which has a character reminiscent of Romanesque churches in the west. Rădăuți is the nucleus of the Romanian province of Bucovina, whose northern extension has formed part of the Soviet Union since 1945. The Soviet frontier can be seen riding the crest of the hills and there are Russian journals for sale at the local kiosks. The older shop-keepers of Rădăuți, born at a time when Bucovina was a province of the Austrian Empire and when German was the foreign language, can recount the extraordinary fluctuations of the town's fortune.

To the north of Suceava, in surroundings of ravishing rustic beauty, is the remarkable monastery of Dragomirna built by the Metropolitan Crîmca of Moldavia in 1609. Crîmca, it appears, was an ambitious man who, in order to outshine Stephen the Great, aspired to build a church at least twice the usual height. The result is a real sensation. Crîmca's church springs like an artesian well from behind its majestic ramparts. Since there are no side-apses to hinder the effect of vertical thrust, the eye is soon arrested by the stone tracery on the tower, as intricate and decorative as some of the doorways of Iberian churches. The Gothic slenderness of this extraordinary building is matched by the sheer mass of the towers which command the wall; the monastery, still in use today, has the air on an impregnable rock rising out of a sea of apple orchards.

In the far north-eastern corner of Romania, at the village formerly called Liveni but now named Enescu is the target of many a modern pilgrimage. This, a small low-roofed house with a wooden balustrade and strings of onions hung to dry in the sun, is where the country's greatest composer, conductor and musician, George Enescu, was born in 1881. His rise to fame was phenomenal and put Romania on the musical map of Europe. At five he was playing the violin and at six started composition. Soon he was to travel to Vienna and Paris, where aged eighteen he won the Conservatoire's Grand Prix for violin and, through contact with teachers such as Massenet and Fauré, took part in that marvellous and mysterious cross-fertilisation of genius. In 1902 Enescu made his début in London and Berlin and formed in Paris his own chamber trio. His work, including the two Romanian Rhapsodies and Suites for Orchestra were as elevated as his early friendships: Casals, Saint-Saens, Ravel, among them.

The passionate virtuoso with an intense and melancholy face that lent itself to caricature embarked on a career of permanent travel. Gustav Mahler conducted his work in New York; younger prodigies like Yehudi Menuhin took lessons from him and joined him in recitals, but for all his international acclaim Enescu's lyrical treatment of folk themes, his epic glorification of Romania's traditions and landscapes and perhaps most of all, his unfailing devotion to his own people made him something of a father-figure, as Bartók in Hungary or Sibelius in Finland. After the Second World War he made very frequent visits to England, America and elsewhere, even conducting at Covent Garden and Glyndebourne and lecturing at Brighton. When he died in 1955, an International Violin Competition was established in his name and five years later the first of the George Enescu International Festivals of music was inaugurated at Bucharest, with Barbirolli, Menuhin and David Oistrakh, among others, taking part. The little house near Dorohoi to which the globetrotting composer-violinist made an annual homecoming is now a National Memorial and an inspiration.

From Suceava to the Maramureṭ area of Transylvania an asphalt highway traverses some of the finest mountain scenery in the country and passes through the spas of Cîmpulung Moldovenesc and Vatra Dornei and several attractive villages where the wooden houses and their carved gates and flower-decked windows and the exquisite local costume give an impression of time standing still. Not far from Cîmpulung are the Pietrele Doamnei, a group of limestone monoliths rising sheer from a forest of conifers. The volcanic structure of these mountains is such that the carbogaseous baths of Vatra Dornei are warm enough for bathers even in winter. From Vatra another road follows the watercourse of the River Bistriṭa with its string of hydropower dams south to the reservoir at Bicaz, Romania's largest inland lake. Near Bicaz a series of stupendous gorges below the mighty massif of Mount Ceahlau barely leave room for the tumultuous River Bicaz as it tumbles eastwards and the tortuous road which man has carved from the grey cliff-face. Just over the watershed, on the Transylvanian side, lies Lăcul Roşu, or Red Lake, which came into being in 1838 when a landslide diverted the river. The white stumps of the old forest still pierce the surface of its water. This lake and its small summer-and-winter resort flanked by pine-studded hills has a pristine peacefulness about it more reminiscent of the New Zealand Alps or Southern Andes than of other European lakes.

Before leaving the Carpathians and entering the steppe-like lands of eastern and southern Moldavia there are three further monasteries of interest to our passionate sightseer, those of Bistriţa and Neamţ near the changing city of Piatra Neamţ and one at Agapia, not far from the market-town of Tîrgu Neamţ. Suffice it to describe but one of them. The Neamţ Monastery is a perfect and historically influential specimen of the Moldavian feudal grouping of church, monks' cells and arcaded and turreted wall which we saw in a highly exaggerated form at Dragomirna. It is greatly to their credit that the Romanians have recently restored it to a good condition.

Between the Rivers Siret and Pruth, the latter demarcating the border with Soviet Moldavia, is a mesopotamia of undulating plateau across which innumerable migrations have passed in history, from the Asian steppe to the melting pot of Europe. Though not spectacular its countryside is pleasant enough and its chief city, Jassy (Iaşi) exceptionally interesting to visit, both as the capital of one of Romania's historic principalities and as a catalyst of recent changes. Its ubiquitous statues, to Alexandru Cuza, the father of modern Romania, to Kogălniceanu the historian and statesman, to the poet Eminescu and writers Ion Creangă and Mihail Sadoveanu, testify to the veneration of culture which is a tradition in Jassy; all these men were born in Moldavia and in the 19th century the city's university and other institutions formed the minds not only of Romania's leadership but also of Greek and Bulgarian patriots, who were to win *their* countries' national independence. For a general impression of Jassy, with its proliferating housing estates, pink and white like the blossoms which embellish the neighbouring countryside in spring, the best panorama unfolds from the hill of Repedea to the south. At night the city is like an immense hearth of burning embers, its industrial areas vibrating, pulsating, the old town blinking, until the fireflies cease to dance in the trees and the city goes to sleep. In the centre of town is the Piaţa Unirii from which all the more interesting sights are within a short distance. The neo-Baroque National Theatre is a good instance of a style found in most of Romania's larger cities, but the neo-Gothic Palace of Culture, formerly the Administrative Palace, is unusual by any criteria. Begun in 1907 by Berindei it is, perhaps, a Balkan answer to St. Pancras Station but better suited to its context. Inside, a group of museums, of fine arts, ethnography, history and science, and a large library are today housed; outside stands an equestrian statue of Stephen the Great. Jassy's Golia Monastery, whose tower gives another view over the city, resembles in form the churches of northern Moldavia but its effect is somewhat anticlimatic as a result. Nobody, however, should miss the Church of the Three Hierarchs (Trei Ierarhi). The interior of this church (1639) with its mosaics of shining gold, its enamelled icons and resplendent candelabra, was decorated mainly by Muscovite craftsmen, but the superb exterior, traced throughout with geometric and arabesque stone mouldings, is the classic synthesis of Moldavian and Caucasian styles. Many of Romania's greatest sons are buried here, including Alexandru Cuza.

In the far south, where Wallachia, Moldavia and the Dobrogea converge on the Danube, are the throbbing port cities of Galaţi and Brăila. Both are major industrial towns today, the former boasting one of the largest steel plants in Europe, but their modernisation is very recent and there are, still living, townsmen who remember the turn-of-the-century dilapidation and abject depression in which both towns acquiesced for many centuries. Only a century ago there were minarets on the southern banks of the Danube where today are rising large housing estates; one traveller recalls the lugubrious cries of the Wallachian harbour-master at Brăila, another the misery of little wooden shacks on the waterfront at Galăţi. These two cities, and particularly Brăila, are still cosmopolitan, partly because of their Greek, Tatar and other colonies but also because of the many ships which sail here, through the Danube Delta, from all parts of the world. At Galăţi they are now building boats for ocean service. There is a hydrofoil service from Brăila and Galăţi to the Delta town of Tulcea, and the myriad islands and clouds of aquatic birds encountered on the way provide an unusual introduction to the Dobrogea.

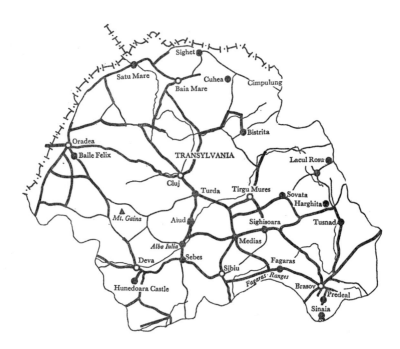

CHAPTER FIVE

Transylvania

*Popular image – History – Fusion of Romanian, Magyar
and Saxon cultures – Folk arts, festivities and customs – Prahova
Valley – Braşo and Poiana Braşov – Făgăraş Mountains –
Mediaeval cities of Sighişoara and Sibiu – Alba Iulia – Dacian
Sarmizegetusa (Gradiştea) – Roman Sarmizegetusa (Ulpia
Trajana) – Deva – Hunedoara – Retezat Mountains – Legend of
Iorgovan's Stone – Tîrgu Mureş – Spas of Sovata and Tuşnad –
Wooden churches of Maramureş – Mountain roads – Cluj –
Natural phenomena of the Apuseni – Oradea.*

Describing long ago Dracula's remote hideaway in the
mountains of Bistriţa, Bram Stoker helped form the foreigner's image of Transylvania. 'The castle', he wrote, 'is on the
very edge of a terrible precipice. A stone falling from the win-
dow would fall a thousand feet without touching anything!
As far as the eye can reach is a sea of green tree-tops, with
occasionally a deep rift where there is a chasm. Here and
there are silver threads where the rivers wind in deep gorges
through the forests . . .' For all the novel's phantom vampires
flitting through the moonbeams, for all the voluptuous dam-
sels with carnivorous teeth, the description of that castle
would be accurate enough today, and other stock ingredients
of the popular picture such as the fervid melodies of gipsy
fiddlers and a scenery now savage, now sylvan, tell much,
though by no means all, of the exotic story of Transylvania.
A Dutch tourist recently entering the Transylvanian city of
Oradea on his first visit to Romania was mildly surprised that

the asphalt road continued on to Cluj; but he was frankly astonished when it continued all the way from Cluj to Bucharest. For Transylvania is modern as well, rich in more than history, folklore and forests. Beneath its fertile soil there is enough salt to supply the whole world for fourteen years, with gold, iron, coal, gas and mercury besides.

As the north-western province of historic Dacia, as the south-eastern march of medieval Hungary and as the massive hinterland of the new Romania, Transylvania has always been a natural fortress girt with mountains. Its name is generally understood to mean most of the territory formally reunited with the Kingdom of Romania in 1920, at Trianon; some would include the Banat within its confines. Arriving from Wallachia or Moldavia the traveller is instantly struck by the differences evident in the towns: high-pitched red roofs and narrow twisting alleyways, and even in the climate, for it is cooler here. Eastern Europe has given way to Central Europe. As varied as the landscape are the people: four million Romanians, one and a half million Magyars, half a million Germans and many Serbs, Slovaks, Bulgars and gypsies. These peoples today reside in a greater harmony and prosperity than was the unfortunate case over the centuries. Although the northern heirs to ancient Dacia lived here, Transylvania was, after a series of fierce encounters, conquered by the Hungarian Kingdom between the 9th and 12th centuries and settled with a Magyar tribe, the Szeklers, who were posted on the eastern and south-eastern frontiers as guards and then by Germans, mainly Saxons, who founded and colonised a number of fortified cities, seven of which (modern Braşov, Cluj, Sibiu, Sighişoara, Sebeş, Bistriţa and Mediaş) gave Transylvania its German name: Siebenbürgen. Magyar nobility were imported as administrators, notwithstanding the fact that the large majority of inhabitants, the indigenous Vlach peasantry had greater affinites with their Wallachian and Moldavian brethren than with the Hungarian and German colonists. In 1600 Michael the Brave,

9. Another view of the Suceviţa Monastery.

19. The 'Pietrele Doamnei' in the Rarău Mountains

11. The ruins of Histria, a 7th century B.C. Greek citadel.

12. The Savings and Deposit Bank in Bucharest.

Voivod of Wallachia, united for one short year all three Romanian Principalities and the memory of this episode inspired and strengthened the cause of Romanian union, which became a reality after the First World War.

The history of Transylvania is as tortuous as its mountain by-ways. During the Reformation the Saxons converted to Lutheranism, the Magyars to Calvinism and the Szeklers to Unitarianism, while in the 18th century most of the Transylvanian Romanians followed their Orthodox Metropolitan into a Uniate Church, formally in submission to Rome but retaining the Orthodox rite, the Uniates returning to the Orthodox fold only in 1948. There were incidents of blood and turmoil as in 1848 when the Romanian peasantry and Saxon fought a bitter war with the Magyar nobility. Following the Austro-Hungarian Compromise of 1867 Transylvania was fully absorbed by Imperial Hungary and the subsequent fifty-year record of exceedingly oppressive Hungarian rule was not a credit to Budapest. Ancient animosities were stirred again in 1940 when Hitler and Mussolini, by the famous Vienna Diktat, retroceded northern Transylvania to their Hungarian allies. Since 1947, when Romania regained her lost territory, much of the strain and stress has happily been removed and the visitor is impressed by the manner in which the Hungarian minority preserves its own cultural life. To this day you will meet Magyar peasants who practise their traditional folk arts and blonde German townspeople proudly cognisant of their medieval provenance. Romanian, naturally enough, is the official tongue but here German is as useful to the foreigner as is French in other parts of the country. Youth, like its counterpart elsewhere, often learns English and in tourist centres such as Poiana Braşov the authorities are sure to have stationed guides conversant not only in English, French and German, but also such languages as Dutch, Swedish, Italian and Spanish.

Transylvanian art is remarkable less for its intrinsic originality than for the persistence, despite Magyar and other in-

81

fluences, of Romanian traditions. The earliest churches, for instance, are a synthesis of Byzantine, Romanesque and Gothic elements, while certain later examples such as the Church of St. Nicholas in Braşov and the 19th- and 20th-century Orthodox cathedrals of several towns display many Moldavian and Brancovan features. One may remark that while Wallachia and Moldavia were primarily concerned with the world of Byzantium, with Ottoman Turkey and Imperial Russia, Transylvania experienced an evolution similar to that of Hungary, the German states and Western Europe in general, fully undergoing the religious upheavals and largely subject to the stylistic trends in architecture and other arts of the Catholic and Protestant countries.

Both the German and Magyar settlers brought special talents and styles; walled cities such as Sighişoara and the folk motifs of Magyar wood-carving are but two eloquent instances of this. Romanian and Magyar woodwork is to Transylvania what the painted churches are to Moldavia; not only wooden churches but dwellings, household and agricultural utensils, doors, lintels, monumental gates, are intricately and most beautifully carved. The Magyars believe that the Transylvanian manner of carving derives from Magyar history in the Asian steppe and Germans will remind you of the proverbial Teutonic predilection for this craft. In fact, as the Romanian art historian G. Oprescu suggests, Transylvanian wood carving is but a part, albeit an outstanding one, of a tradition common to many forested areas of the Carpathians, of the Danube and the Rhineland. There is a fine range of carved objects in the Ethnological Museum at Cluj: iconostases, furniture, jugs, ladles, gourds, pails, distaffs, spindles, ox-yokes, all being the work of patient village peasants and lonely shepherds in the hills.

Wood-carving is still today a lively art. In the churchyard of Săpinţa, a village of northern Maramureş, one wood carver has carved verse on the wooden crosses of the recently departed. Cut on each cross are representations of the late villager's life. If a man hunted he was carved hunting; if a woman was known to be industrious she was shown spinning; if a villager was drunk he was depicted with a bottle in his hand and an appropriate line of verse beneath. On one cross the hammer and sickle denotes membership of the Communist Party. As a finishing touch the philosopher-artist has inscribed on the wooden entrance gate the words: 'A Cemetery of Folk Art'.

Ceramics, embroidery and tapestry likewise flourish. Their geometric designs have been traced back to the inhabitants of all south-east Europe, Thracian tribes who in turn owed much to their Stone and Bronze Age ancestors.

Folk festivities, closely linked to nature and the basic phenomena of life: birth, marriage and death, are especially vital and original in Transylvania. Many customs date back to Dacian times but, born of the practical experience of shepherd and peasants, they reflect the native wit and spiritual needs of all ages. The folk tradition here, as so often, tends to have a lay character, closely linked to life. At New Year there are ceremonies known as *plugușor* ('small plough'), *capra* ('goat') and *sorcova* ('paper-flowers') symbolising peasant hopes for a rich harvest, health and happiness. In spring it is a custom to celebrate the *sîmbra oilor* when shepherds leave for the mountains with their flocks, or the vivid *drăgaica* at which men dressed up as women and carrying swords and flags perform an ancient dance. Travelling in the 1930's Walter Starkie was told by Saxon peasants in Sibiu that they would dance before the church as a plea for good harvests. The performers must dance faster and faster so that sweat would stream down their faces, for perspiration was a symbol of rain, which fertilises the fields. The most popular dances of Transylvania are the *fecioreasca*, *hațegana*, *ardeleana* and variations of the *invîrtita*, the latter being a whirl dance characterised by a halting rhythm known as *aksak*. As a rule instrumental dance tunes are accompanied by waggish rhymes improvised by the performers as they dance. Romanian music thrills the heart by its alternation of gay and melancholic melody. The *hora*, danced in a grave and dignified circle by all the village, is performed throughout the land and the most expressive of the songs of the Romanians is the plaintive *doina*, richly ornamented with arabesques and deeply evocative of the past.

Another genre of the Transylvanian, indeed of the Romanian, oral tradition in music is the ballad in narrative style extolling the heroics of former ages or recounting ancient legends. Contemporary themes, however, are by no means ignored and youth may prefer the Beatles. In the autumn, when unfermented wine flows freely at the wayside *mustărie*, a merry band of Bacchic youngsters adapts the latest pop and jazz to the folk idiom of their fathers. Every year festivals of folk music are held at the resorts of the Prahova Valley, as in Bucharest and Mamaia, but many country towns and villages in Transylvania stage less elaborate performances for their own amusement. Typical instruments, some of them of untold antiquity, range from pear-tree leaves, birch bark and fish-scales to mountain horns, kobsas, trumpets, bagpipes, whistles, flutes, pan-pipes and hammered dulcimers.

Funeral customs have also retained their ancient lay form. The old ritual songs such as *zorile* ('dawn') and *cîntecul cel mare* ('the great song') are still recited in western Transylvania and the north of Oltenia while in part of Moldavia a burial wake figure is performed by masked dancers. All over Romania, the wailing that accompanies a funeral as a last farewell to the dead often takes the form of a dirge in which an improvised conversation is held with the deceased.

Fairs are another occasion for celebration, when peasants from different villages meet to sing and dance, and many have changed but little since the Middle Ages. One of the best in Transylvania is the Maidens' Fair, held on Mt. Găina in the Apuseni Mountains on the 20th July, when peasants from the Bihor, Alba and Cluj districts come to sell their woodware, pottery and fruit and to dance and rejoice in one another's company. By custom the local girls assemble here to meet their future husbands. In a glorious setting of brilliant colours, infectious rhythms and the excited chatter of the crowd, Mt. Găina is unforgettable.

On Harvest Day, the 1st October, the majority of towns celebrate nature's bounty: eggplants and grapes, peppers, plums and pumpkins are sold for a song: tame bears dance and romp in the street and, in Transylvania, the country lads, their black boots hung with bells and their girl-friends embellished with flowery bonnets, parade *en masse* in the costume of the region.

Transylvania is also mountain country. In the Apuseni there is human habitation up to the 4,000 foot mark and one sees villages crowning the hilltops. For communication they invented the *tulnic*, a local kind of Alpenhorn. Though Romanian agriculture consists over-ridingly of co-operatives and state farms you will find individual smallholdings in those mountain areas where collectivisation is difficult. Many places are so thickly wooded that man finds himself a stranger overwhelmed by the dark and timeless company of firs and spruce shooting ever upward in their search for the heavens. Even birds are hushed here and the supreme silence of the Carpathian forest can be frightening. Often ferns and a tangled undergrowth give cover to deer, bear, wild boar and other animals, and in winter the howling of wolves is not un-common.

Probably the most dramatic approach to Transylvania is from the south through the Prahova Valley. From Ploieşti the plain recedes rapidly, the valley steepens, conifers, larch, beech cluster ever closer to the rising banks; a view of craggy peaks appears through the wet mist and suddenly you are in an Alpine landscape under a cobalt sky. You have reached Sinaia, the Pearl of the Carpathians, resort town and spa that could be mistaken for Marienbad were it not for the fanciful villas in the Wallachian style and the mountain chalets poised on the hillside. Sinaia's casino is modelled on that of Monte Carlo and its main street, lined with trees and cafés, exhales the very spirit of the 19th century. Although it first made headlines as the summer residence of King Carol I, Sinaia dates back to the late 17th century when Mihail Cantacuzino commemorated his pilgrimage to Mt. Sinai by erecting a monastery. The old church is a tiny Brancovan gem set inside a whitewashed cloister. Its west porch has frescoes showing a 'Stream of Fire' recalling Voroneţ and, as the early morning dew evaporates on the windows and the rising sun lights up the wooded mountainside, a scattering of the faithful fill the pronaos and, in the naos, monks with glazed eyes and a big-boned gypsy soprano intone the matins. In the cloister stands a decorous and simple chapel, its murals dimmed with age, its iconostasis carved to crude effect. The bigger 19th-century church to the side is less prepossessing but the interior is resplendent with gilt frescoes and a gigantic iconostasis in the Byzanto-Wallachian style.

Many Romanians and foreigners come to Sinaia and who would not like to live here? One Romanian couple has brought, on a fifteen-year credit out of their factory earnings, a charming two-storey Alpine house, taking in paying guests and being the soul of warmth and courtesy, even to the extent of preparing tea for Englishmen.

A road winds through an informal garden to the Castle of Peleş (1875), a florid and magnificent configuration of German Baroque, Renaissance and Alpine components with marble sculptures, timbered balustrades and fantastic tapering turrets. Devised originally for King Carol I, its air of German hunting-lodge makes obvious concessions to his Hohenzollern background; the interior rooms, now forming a museum, lead off from a massive veneered wood staircase to a wealth of paintings, carpets, period furniture, armour and weapons, while in the gardens are two smaller buildings, Pelişor and, after a Swiss model, the Foisor Tower.

Continuing up the Prahova Valley one reaches three other resorts: Buşteni, Azuga and Predeal. Here the dizzy sentinels of the Prahova, the peaks of Caraiman and Omul, tower to 8,000 feet above the floor of the valley, their grandeur enhanced by the snow of winter. At Azuga you will find what the Romanians call *izbuc*, rapid springs of water running deep into underground lakes. The town's drinking water, supplied from such a source, tends to taste of stone. The mountains rising on the western side of the Prahova are the Bucegi, a high but compact massif which, thanks to numerous tracks and chair-lifts are accessible to hikers in summer and skiers in winter. A long but memorable walk over the shoulder of Omul leads to one of the most romantic Gothic fortresses in Europe, Castle Bran, built by Hansa merchants in the 14th century and for long inhabited by German knights. Never conquered by the Turks it functioned as a toll station between Transylvania and Wallachia and is now a museum.

At the head of the Prahova Valley the resort of Predeal straddles the watershed of the Carpathians. The trains halt here for a few minutes as if to breathe the ozone. The highest hill-town in the country, Predeal is in search of a Romanian Osbert Lancaster: its marvellous Mincuesque villas with their fantasy towers and belvederes, their latticed dormer-windows and conical roofs, do not yet appear on the pages of guide books. Predeal coasts on its reputation as a ski centre.

After Predeal the train winds downhill suddenly to emerge in the Transylvanian Plain. Here, nestling under the formidable bulk of Mt. Tîmpa, is Braşov, Romania's second city, in terms of size and industry, a city schizophrenically but happily divided between medieval and late 20th century, as one soon perceives on alighting at the ultra-modern railway station. The old town is comfortably compact and is dominated by the largest and most important Gothic, and Catholic church in Romania, the Black Church (Biserica Neagra), so called on account of a fire two centuries back which reduced it to a few charred walls.

In the Schei quarter or old Romanian ghetto, is the Orthodox Church of St. Nicholas, built in 1595 in the Wallachian manner and later transformed by the addition of various Gothic Renaissance and Baroque elements. As a symbol of Romanian Orthodoxy it enjoyed the benefactions of Wallachian and Moldavian voivods and its clock-tower (1751) was a gift of the Empress Elizabeth of Russia. In the courtyard stands the building which housed the first Romanian School in 1595, now an historical museum.

The charmingly low gabled houses of old Brasov sometimes harbour eating places of an excellent standard. One such, the Cerbul Carpatin ('Carpathian Stag'), sunk in a medieval cellar near the Black Church, epitomises, with its barrel-vaulted ceiling, folk themes and spirited music, the Transylvanian style of dining. More cosmopolitan is the new Hotel Carpaţi which has an elegance and purity of line rare for any country.

Buses follow a good highway up to the resort of Poiana Braşov which, equipped with many hotels, villas, chalets and clubs, is in summer a beautiful base for cool walks in mountain and forest and in winter a sparkling snowscape of horse-driven sleighs and live Christmas trees. It is Romania's best known ski resort and the scene of international competitions. A little further from Brasov is Prejmer, a wonderful 15th-century peasant citadel centred around a Romanesque church. In times of siege the inner walls of its fortress provided shelter for nearly 300 peasants. There is another fortified village of the same period at Hărman, with a particularly impressive grey church quite encompassed by the sturdy walls.

Not far to the west of Braşov loom the Făgăraş Mountains. At the heart of the range, Moldoveanul and Negoiul, both over 8,000 feet, are the highest peaks in the Romanian Carpathians and the escarpment on the northern side resembles a great wall stretched against the sky. The Făgăraş are studded with seventy glacial lakes, known locally as 'eyes of the sea', one of which, Lake Giurgiului, is so chilly that the water never rises above freezing point. In the higher crevices snow

lingers well into midsummer but a surprising variety of vegetation is found, making these mountains a paradise for
scientists, walkers and winter-sportsmen. The southern foothills are carpeted with deciduous forests of beech, oak and
sycamore, a perfect refuge for wild boar which, on tiring of a
diet of acorns and beechnuts, invade the tidy plots of the hill
farmers below. Far up in the Alpine zone the little life that
exists must literally bow to the wind – and the small but
hardy mountain spruce have a sculptured beauty about them.

North of the Făgăraş are the picturesque cities of Sighişoara
and Sibiu, founded by Saxons in the early Middle Ages. Of
all Romanian towns, Sighişoara is the perfect realisation of a
medieval *Burg* huddled around its citadel and monastery.
The chief attractions are the Church on the Hill in the late
Gothic style, reached by a flight of 172 steps, and the 14th-
century clock-tower with a clock, dating from 1648, whose
mechanism sets in motion seven carved figures, each repre-
senting a day of the week. The citadel has been left practically
untouched by the passing of time and remains a complete
ensemble of undulating walls and bastions: the Ropers'
Tower, Butchers' Tower, Furriers' Tower, Tailors' Tower,
Bootmakers' Tower, Tanners' Tower and the bizarre 14th-
century Tinsmiths' Tower, whose ground floor is rectangular,
middle floors pentagonal, top floor octagonal and roof hex-
agonal. The modern town has been allowed to grow up be-
side the ancient fortress and has blended well.

Considerably bigger is Sibiu which, like Braşov, consists of
medieval and modern sectors. Parts of its walls remain and
the flying buttresses of the Passage of the Steps recall the Via
Dolorosa of Crusader Jerusalem. Sibiu's Gothic Reformed
Church is strikingly monumental. But the most celebrated
spot in Sibiu is the Brukenthal Museum, one of the oldest in
Europe and named after an 18th-century governor of Transylvania whose collection, housed in his own Baroque man-
sion, was opened to the public in 1817. It possesses the widest
assortment of ethnographic, historical and scientific objects

and also masterpieces by Flemish, Dutch, German and Venetian painters – Rubens, Van Dyck, Van Eyck, Titan and Veronese among them.

A third town of the middle plain is Alba Iulia which, though not large, has been inhabited continuously since neolithic times. Known to the Romans as Apulum and to Slavs as Belgrad ('white city'), Alba Iulia has been prominent in the history of Romania, for in the 17th century many of the first publications in the Romanian language were printed here and in 1785 two of the leaders of the 1784 peasant revolt, Horia and Cloşca were broken on the wheel outside the town and the third, Crişan, killed himself in his cell. Then in 1918 a Great Popular Assembly opted for Transylvania's union with the Old Kingdom of Romania and four years later King Ferdinand and Queen Marie were symbolically crowned in Alba Iulia's Orthodox Cathedral, a church designed in Brancovan style. The old centre still preserves a Catholic Cathedral spanning five centuries of construction and an 18th-century citadel built by 20,000 serfs under the supervision of Prince Eugene of Savoy.

You cannot travel far in Transylvania without confronting mountains. To the stark highlands of the Retezat, the usual route from Alba Iulia is by way of the Mureş Valley, passing Simeria, with its 250 year old arboretum, planted with trees from all parts of the globe, to Deva, principal town of the region. But no one can now miss the opportunity of two détours to the chief Dacian and Roman sites in Romania.

In the mountain fastness south of Orăştie the archaeologists, long acquainted with a number of ruined fortresses and settlements in the district, have concluded that it was here – and not further west at the Roman site of Sarmizegetusa – that King Decebal, the heroic Dacian war leader who till the year 106 A.D. resisted Trajan's legionaries, in fact resided. The Dacian Sarmizegetusa, now called the Gradiştea Citadel, raised on a terraced plateau at a cool and often windswept height of 4,000 feet, has as majestic a setting as any ancient mountain city west of the Persian Ecbatana. Much excavation has still to be made but two circular sanctuaries, whose monoliths served as a time-calendar and call to mind Stonehenge, four rectangular sanctuaries and several other establishments are easily identified and stylistically quite distinctive. If this was really the royal capital of the Dacians, the original Sarmizegetusa, as evidence leads us to suppose, then further digging should bring to light a good deal of material, not only on Decebal, who is the Romanian equivalent of Vercingetorix or Boadicea, but also on the remarkable culture of the Dacians.

The Roman city of Sarmizegetusa, lying on the main road from Hateg to Timişoara, has been much more thoroughly excavated though even here there is still more to be unearthed. When the two protracted campaigns of the Emperor Trajan had finally reduced the Dacians, the Romans were not content merely to consolidate their gains by maintaining a military presence, for since Dacia was an exceptionally valuable acquisition (it supported a thriving agriculture and was to yield much gold and copper), the Romans found the province an ideal one for settlement. Legionaries and ordinary citizens from all over the civilised world were, during the subsequent century of Roman rule, to migrate to this remote outpost, Romanising the Dacians and laying the foundations, especially in language, of the modern Romania.

In the year 110 A.D. Rome founded on this site Colonia Ulpia Trajana. Protected by a great wall, parts of which have survived, the city included the Aedes Augustalium, the largest palace of its kind in the provinces of the Empire, an amphitheatre for gladiatorial games, the only example in Romania and in good condition, a forum and many dwellings. A walk about the courtyards of former houses will reveal pieces of columns and various decorative mouldings suggestive of the luxuries of Romano-Dacian life at Ulpia Trajana, and the museum exhibits a splendid assortment of reliefs, architectural fragments and artefacts.

Both at Deva and at neighbouring Hunedoara the fortifications are visible reminders of the troubled history of the Hunedoara Transylvanians and the ferocity of their resistance to invaders. On its pyramidal hill the ruined fortress of Deva commands a generous view of the valley and surrounding mountains: the savage skyline of the Retezat to the south and, in the opposite direction, the milder and sinuous shapes of the Apuseni, while at Hunedoara, now a major steel city, the castle with its motley towers and gables and its lofty drawbridge evoke the fantasy world of Grimm. Hunedoara Castle is forever bound up with the immortal memory of Iancu of Hunedoara who stemmed the Ottoman tide, with his son Matthias Corvinus who was to become one of Hungary's greatest kings and later with Gabriel Bethlen, a distinguished Prince of Transylvania. It impresses the romantic imagination at least as indelibly as the famous Alcazar at Segovia and yet is scarcely if at all known in the west!

The Retezat Mountains tyrannise the landscape below Hunedoara; neither road nor railway can penetrate them but have laboriously to follow their lower, though by no means unspectacular eastern flanks, to enter Oltenia through the narrow dale of the River Jiu. On account of their sheer and ragged silhouette, the Retezat are sometimes termed the Transylvanian Alps and their history is worth the telling. During the glaciations of the tertiary period, great masses of frozen snow carved deep cauldrons and steep-walled basins in the ancient plateau. As the glaciers started streaming towards the valleys below, screes loosened from the rocky slopes and, falling into the glacier, were dragged down to the 3,000 foot level where the moraines formed towering heaps of boulders as soon as the glaciers melted. Then, thanks to the stresses of extreme changes in temperature, huge blocks of stone were dislodged and rolled down the mountainside so that today walking over the screes is a difficult and sometimes dangerous exercise.

In the Retezat lie more than eighty glacial lakes. The best

known is Lake Bucura, Romania's biggest Alpine lake, but there are many others of interest such as Lake Gemenele, lost in a thicket of dwarf conifers and rare cembran pines. Those who have climbed to these isolated sheets of water will be well rewarded, for the first sight of the lake from the higher ridges of its basin is quite breathtaking. Then, clambering down the scree they can rest and bathe in the lake, pass the night under a ledge and, round a fire of dwarf pine branches, wait for the magical moment at sunrise when the encircling cliffs are suddenly mirrored in the dark water, its surface sometimes broken by rising trout. Foaming torrents and waterfalls feed the lakes and rivers, forming majestic defiles such as that of the River Cerna.

Near the source of the Cerna, in the hill hamlet of Soarbele the shepherds can recount the legendary origin of a limestone colossus called Iorgovan's Stone. There was once, according to them, a dragon who used to swallow young maidens in a single gulp. After consuming a dozen local maidens it came the turn of the Emperor's daughter. The Emperor had built a castle in Transylvania at a spot which is today named Subcetate – people passing that way may still see the ruins near the summit with a razed top called Retezatul. It seems that the Emperor himself had taken a slice off the peak to gain a clear view of the dragon's approach and thus protect his daughter. Whereupon the disgruntled monster turned tail and reached Soarbele where it swallowed a herd of oxen and a whole flock of sheep, shepherd and all. It happened that a brave knight named Iorgovan who was passing by resolved to challenge the dragon, but not until he had acquired a magnificent sword from a famous gypsy smith. The weapon was so strong that, when Iorgovan tested it on the stone now bearing his name the rock was cleft in two and water issued forth. Armed with this magic sword our hero chased the dragon and cut off its tail, then, pursuing it all the way down the Cerna Valley, he chopped off bits of the hideous creature until all that remained was its head.

The exceedingly rich and diverse vegetation of the Retezat has spread even to the most inaccessible of rocky salients. Animals abound; packs of wolves roam the southern slopes and wild boar, rooting for crocus bulbs, leave numerous holes in the earth. Bear even forsake their vegetarian diet to sample fresh mutton, causing great losses to shepherds whose flocks can graze in these parts only two or three months in the year. The lynx, whose Romanian translation is *rîs*, meaning 'smile', makes its lair in hillside caves and chamois, as agile as acrobats, negotiate the steepest crags, leaping across yawning chasms and vanishing with amazing speed. The chamois love salt and, before tourism developed here, groups of them would be seen on fine autumn days approaching the lakes to lick the lumps of salt left for them by gamekeepers. In spring, nonetheless, the chamois and their young can still be seen sunning themselves on the remotest pinnacles and, in early May, the walker who reaches the forester's hut at Cîmpuşel, near the sources of the Jiu and Cerna, will discern these mountain antelopes peacefully browsing along the narrow ledges of Dîlma Cu Brazi. Much of the Retezat has been made a National Park, with certain zones reserved exclusively for scientists.

Moving now to the very heartland of Transylvania we come to another but very different mountainous territory whose population includes the densest concentration of Magyars in Romania. Tîrgu Mureş, the principal town, called Maros Vasarhély by Hungarian speakers, is a clean and bustling place with a very spacious main street liberally planted with flower-beds and conifers. The citizens, who are proud of their culture, will point out to you the Teleki Library with its 40,000 volumes, many of them incunabula and rare printings, and the Bolyai Museum named after the Magyar geometer, János Bolyai. The Museum of History illustrates the eventful story of the area.

Roads radiating east from here soon ascend the thickly forested foothills of the Gurghiu and Harghita Ranges, the longest volcanic chain, now extinct, in Europe. In the supple folds of the mountains are small villages and several gleaming lakes. A famous spa, Sovata, which is practically engulfed by the wooden mountains thrives on its deposits of rock-salt and its remarkable sun-heated pools. The largest pool, Lake Ursu, is saline because its trough lies in a mountain of sodium chloride. The water is warm but, in contrast to other such places, has a thin layer of fresh water literally floating on the surface and emanating from two small streams. It is indeed a strange sensation to feel, when standing in this lake, a collar of fresh cold water about one's neck and shoulders while the lower parts of the body are bathed by salt water that gets progressively warmer the further down one goes. Sovata is a base for many hikes along the hills and, zig-zagging for two hours, a small mountain train rides up Mt. Saca where a glorious panorama unfolds, of the Transylvanian Plateau and Făgăraş Mountains. Again, a delightful country road up the Sebeş Valley leads through hazel groves and raspberry canes to the old trout hatchery at Trocuţa. The fisherman is spoiled for choice in the Gurghiu.

Not far from the Moldavian border and crouching in a gorge of the upper Olt is the spa of Tuşnad. The uplands of the Harghita to the west, like the Gurghiu and Giurgeu Ranges, hold special interest for the scientist since the craters of their dead volcanoes are filled with bogs of moss and peat, yielding many plant and animal relics of the glacial period. The swamps are often fringed with groves of spruce, alder and beech trees and their charm is enhanced by small round or oval lakes, deep and clear, which seem perpetually to pursue their greenish lips.

The Mohoş bog, lining the crevices of an old volcano above Tuşnad, is known to natives as *Locul Cu Coacaze*, or place of red currants and bilberries, on account of its luxurious vegetation. Unusually deep is the Lake of St. Anne (Sfînta Ana) lying in a crater at 3,000 feet. The St. Anne of local legend was a young woman who, pursued by a tyrant, cursed him so that his castle was swallowed up by the earth. In its place the lake appeared and the villain is said to swim beneath its waters in the guise of a dragon, while the maiden lives again in the forget-me-nots of the lakeside.

One province in the far north of Romania deserving of greater attention than has been given it by foreigners is Maramureş. Its highways are few but certainly afford adequate access to its picturesque and tranquil countryside. Neither Baia Mare, today a prosperous centre of the non-ferrous metals industry, nor the lumbering town of Satu Mare is especially distinguished, but a third town Sighet (Sightul Marmaţiei), wrapped in a quilt of woods and orchards a mile or two from the Soviet frontier, makes a good base for seeing the exquisite wooden churches of Maramureş. There may be one thousand wood-built churches all over Transylvania, but those of Maramureş, by dint of their simple beauty, are unparalleled. To the south are the 18th-century churches of Sişeşti, Bineşti, Păuliş, Surdeşti and Plopiş, and also, near Lăpuş, a 16th-century church at Rogoz, the slender spire at Surdeşti actually attaining a height of 180 feet.

On another road from Sighet, which threads along the Iza Valley, are even more numerous wooden churches, the best of which are in the villages of Rozavlea, Ieud and Cuhea. Some of these buildings contain no iron or stone in their structures, being put together with wooden nails, and the little Biserica Dintrun Lemn, meaning 'church out of wood', was hewn from the solid truck of one oak tree. They possess wonderfully and elaborately carved porches, windows and even candelabra; seen in the strong sunlight, something mysterious is suggested by the broad shadows cast by the low penthouse roofs; the dark wood imparts a solemn weight to the structure and the fine steeples, exceedingly high in relation to the squat mass of the rest, give a quaint but most pleasing appearance to the whole. And in the summery meadows the cone-shapes of the haystacks seem to echo the contour of the churches. Sighet, by the way, has a well-endowed Ethnographical Museum.

The motorist travelling in the direction of Moldavia is here faced with an exacting choice between two mountain roads of the utmost magnificence. The more direct highway from Sighet passes the timber mills of Vişeul-de-Sus and a scattering of pretty villages till it reaches the little town of Moisei, which has a beautiful 18th-century monastery. Further east this road rises to Prislop (with an unusual stone church) and Prislop Pass, nearly 5,000 feet up, snaking down again to the valley of the River Bistriţa as far as the spa of Vatra Dornei. An alternative route proceeds first to the Saxon city of Bistriţa, on the way skirting the rugged Rodna Mountains, and then climbs up to the Tihuţa Pass (4,000 feet) which forms a saddle between the Rodna and equally wild Călimani Massifs. Dracula's Castle was envisaged set amidst the impregnable crags and pine forests of the Bistriţa Valley and in fact the road traditionally figured as the main trade artery between Transylvania and Moldavia.

If Braşov is Romania's second manufacturing city, then second only to Bucharest in culture is Cluj. Walk through the Piaţa Libertăţii dominated by its equestrian statue of Matthias Corvinus and you can still sense, from the slow moving crowd which fills the great square, from the clarion notes of the churchbells and from the countless cafés, the leisurely amplitude of local life. The pedestrian crossing the main streets at midday or in the evening finds himself caught up in a throng of students. The celebrated Babeş-Bolyai University of Cluj is an amalgam of the former Romanian and Magyar Universities, most of its courses now being bilingual. Outside the main lecture-rooms stands a sculpture of the she-wolf suckled by Romulus and Remus. A plaque, reading ALLA CITTA DI CLVJ ROMA MADRE MCMXXI, hints at the cultural rôle of this great Transylvanian city. Even the menu at the Brasserie Continental on the square, formerly the Café New York, offers an appetising fusion of two cuisines. But Romanian and Hungarian speakers maintain their separate theatres, opera, newspapers and books, and the many churches reflect the dual personality of Cluj. The 14th-century Gothic Church of St. Michael, done in whitish stone, is an obvious link with the Catholic west; in a more intimate quarter the old buttressed Reformed Church, in late-Gothic style, forms a handsome ensemble with the Reformed College, and the gleaming Orthodox Cathedral, fashioned as late as 1933 after the neo-Byzantine manner – all betoken the cultural changes that have accompanied the history of this town.

The Ethnographical Museum of Cluj, in the Strada 30 Decembrie, is well assembled and absorbing; not only costumes and implements but even various folk occupations, from mining to pottery, are documented in clearest detail. Cluj also has its own, Transylvanian, 'village museum' in the suburb of Hoia. Up the hill behind the University there is a Botanical Garden whose beds and conservatories display a world-wide collection of plants, including even a Japanese Garden, and it is interesting to see that the botanists correspond with Kew and other foreign equivalents.

From Cluj it is but a short distance to Turda which, from the 16th century, was a seat of the Diet of the Transylvanian Principality and is consequently the repository of many good buildings. But Turda is better known for its gorges where the river is flanked by steep cliffs of limestone. It was here, during the Turkish penetration of Central Europe, that *haiduks*, outlaw patriots corresponding to the modern guerrillas, found safety in the caves and crannies up the rock-face.

This area is the beginning of the Apuseni Mountains, a range of marble and calcium sculpted in the glacial period into strange forms and, since then, further eroded by the elements. Their outline is relatively gentle but the karst phenomena: natural caves and tunnels, buttes and buttresses, vie for grandeur with those of the Dinaric Alps and the American West. Most dramatic of the caves are at the Scări-şoara Glacier, situated on a plateau in the heart of the mountains. One enters them by way of a huge moss-carpeted funnel which descends into an abyss with vertical walls and a lush but weird vegetation of flowering plants. The bottom of this funnel is covered by snow which seldom melts and one reaches a series of gigantic grottoes of which the first, with its domed roof, is the glacier's principal attraction. Countless stalagmites of ice can be made out in the dim light, their carved and translucent columns refracting the light into myriad rays that flicker in the semi-darkness.

There are many other fascinating things in these mountains: suffice it to mention the Cetaţile Ponorului, a natural citadel balanced over a labyrinth of underground caves and streams, the Meziad cave with its five levels of stalagtites, and the extraordinary Focul Viu ('living fire') whose glacial chimney facing the west glows like a furnace at sunset.

The villages of the Apuseni are full of life, some of their methods of house-building having changed little since the days when local gold-panners helped boost the Roman exchequer. In July the roads leading to the gold-mining village of Baia de Criş will be thronged with peasants on their way to the Maidens' Fair on Mt. Găina.

Oradea, situated within a few miles of Hungary on the main road and railway between Cluj and Budapest is the much modernised capital of Bihor county. Its links with the west have been strong ever since its medieval fortress, later supplemented by additions on the models of Vauban, helped defend the Hungarian marches from Turkish encroachments. Oradea has many 18th-century Baroque buildings such as the Episcopal Palace (based on Vienna's Belvedere), the Catholic Cathedral and the Moon Church (Biserica Cu Lună) whose tower displays a clockwork sphere indicating the phases of the moon. In the town Museum you can inspect several engravings of Albrecht Dürer, whose father was born nearby, also one of the world's finest ornithological collections: birds, books about birds, stamps and eggs. To the south-east of the town is the much frequented thermal spa of Băile Felix whose radioactive properties treat a great variety of ailments. In the small river debouching from the lake at Băile Felix there grows a unique and enormous species of water-lily, the *castalea thermalis*, which, thanks to the warmth of the water, is a living relic of the tertiary age. For most travellers from north-western Europe Oradea is the gateway to Romania and, though not an end in itself, it is a pleasant enough spot for a night's rest.

Aråd

Sinicolau Mare

Timisoara

Lugoj

THE BANAT AND OLTENIA

Tirgu Jiu

Govora

Baile Herculane

Turnu Severin

Dragasani

Craiova

CHAPTER SIX

The Banat and Oltenia

*Turbulent history of the Banat – Mingling of peoples –
Timişoara – Plains and mountains – Winter resorts near
Caransebeş – Gypsies – Băile Herculane and the Domogled Nature
Reserve – Cazane Gorges and transformation at the Iron Gates –
Turnu-Severin – Legacy of Rome in Dacia – Oltenia art and
architecture – Oltenian rugs – Tîrgu Jiu – Constantin Brancusi, his
life and work – Tristan Tzara and Eugène Ionesco – Craiova old
and new – Flood-plains of the Danube – Olt Valley, its natural
beauty, its monasteries and saps – Future visitors to Romania.*

The last provinces to claim our attention, the Banat and
Oltenia, offer in several respects a microcosm of Romania, by
virtue not only of their past, but of their topography and
climate. Inhabited since palaeolithic times, the Banat has
throughout history been a cross-roads of migrating peoples,
as much an arena of wars and conflicting claims as Belgium
in the north of Europe. The neolithic discoveries in the Yugoslav part of the Banat have already been alluded to in a
previous chapter but the town Museum at Timişoara shows
archaeological materials at least as old from the eastern parts
of the region. During the Roman period the Banat was
Romanised like the rest of the Dacian province but following
the imperial withdrawal of the 3rd century it was swept by
waves of migrants, some of whom came to plunder, others to
settle. Goths, Huns, Avars, then in the 5th century Slavs and
in the 9th century Magyars infiltrated the western lands of
the Romano-Dacians, joining with the latter population to

resist later Tatar and Turkish onslaughts. After the heroic but catastrophic Battle of Kossovo in 1389 which, as every Serb knows, spelled the end of the Serbian Kingdom and the beginning of six centuries of Ottoman rule over Serbia, many Serbs removed to what was then the Hungarian Banat. The term 'Banat' was, incidentally, used in Hungary to denote a military district; it derives not from the Hungarian but from a Persian word meaning 'overlord' brought to Europe by the Avars.

Mohamed Pasha Sokollu, the illustrious Sokolovich who had been born a Slav and inducted as a child into Turkish service, rising in the course of his extraordinary life from lowly scullion to Grand Vizir, in 1552 took possession of Timişoara and turned the Banat into a *pashalik*, thus extending the boundaries of the yet dynamic Ottoman realm to the gates of Buda itself. Then, as a consequence of the Peace of Passarowitz (1718) the Turks were forced to yield the Banat, along with part of Oltenia, to the victorious Austrians who now established the 'Banat of Temesvar' under a *GeneralKommandant* residing in Timişoara. It is from this period that the large German minority dates, for the Hapsburgs as a matter of policy settled large numbers of Rhineland Germans, mainly Swabians, to till the fertile lands of their new acquisition. Even today the Germans of the Banat retain a quite separate identity from their Saxon cousins in Transylvania, speaking the mellow dialect of the Swabian *Bauer*.

The Austrians confronted the Turks anew in 1738, losing Oltenia to the latter but keeping the Banat. In 1779 the Banat was incorporated into Hungary until in 1849, following the suppression of the Hungarian Revolution, it was merged with the Serbian provinces of Srem and Bačka to form the Austrian-administered 'Serbian Voivodina'. Like a shuttlecock in a game of badminton, the Banat once again reverted to Hungary after the Austro-Hungarian 'Compromise' of 1867. Although ever since the Roman period they had constituted a majority in the Banat, the Romanians, together with the Serb and German minorities, now underwent the same kind of subjection to Budapest as their brethren in Transylvania. The Paris Peace Treaty of 1919 finally resolved the tripartite tug-of-war by conceding the eastern and largest part of the Banat to Romania, together with Transylvania, while the new Kingdom of Yugoslavia acquired a one-third share, the Hungarians retaining the Magyar city of Szeged.

There is much today in this province to recall the events and mingling of cultures on this ancient battleground. While the folk music on the one hand has been nurtured on the influence of the many peoples, their different languages and other cultural attributes persist in such a way as to merit the metaphor of *macédoine* rather than 'melting pot'. The cities of Timişoara and Arad, today bustling centres of engineering and textile manufacturing, whose populations have doubled in thirty years, are probably the most multinational, multicultural towns of their size in Europe. Timişoara, located one hundred miles from Belgrade, supports not only a Romanian culture but also German and Magyar State Theatres, a superb Serbian Dance Ensemble and several Serbian newspapers. At Arad a Romanian Folk Ensemble and the impressive monument to the heroes of the 1848 Revolution do not appear to diminish the rôle of the non-Romanian minorities.

Timişoara has a particularly tormented past, though if you judge from the extensive post-war construction and the verdant stretches along the Bega Canal which bisects the city, you would never guess it. The town Museum, housed in the 14th-century Castle of Iancu of Hunedoara, begins to illustrate this point. There are detailed records of the Roman occupation of Dacia: tablets, inscriptions, coins and so on, also medieval texts documenting the horrors of the 1514 peasant uprising when Gheorghe Doja, its leader, suffered the kind of atrocities which will be known to readers of Ivo Andrić's *Bridge on the Drina*. If in Bosnia the art of impaling had reached its absolute refinement, then the death of Gheorghe Doja was a gruesome novelty. Seated on a throne of burning iron, he was crowned with a hot molten headpiece and then dismembered, his severed limbs subsequently hung on the gates of Oradea, Alba Iulia and Buda as a deterrent to other insurgents.

Half the Romanian Banat is composed of flat and fecund farmland, an extension of the great Pannonian Plain which, drained by the Danube, gives Hungary and northern Serbia the relief and economic aspect of a breadbasket. Prosperous country towns such as Sînicolau Mare, where Bela Bartók was born differ but little in outward appearance from places across the Hungarian frontier, and the rich summer patchwork of maize, sugar-beet, wheat, tobacco, sunflowers and vineyards basking in the hot sun is a picture common enough in Central Europe. But the mountains of the Banat attain the remarkable height of 7,500 feet and are favoured by winter sports enthusiasts till late spring. If you continue up the Timiş Valley through the mottled green plantations of mulberry trees and the silk town of Lugoj you will rise to the lumber capital of Caransebeş which makes a base for wonderful excursions into the backwoods of the Banat, the Semenic and Tarcu Massifs of the Western Carpathians. A narrow-gauge railway scales the flanks of Mt. Tarcu itself while ski slopes abound on the more northerly hulk of Muntele Mic (6,000 feet). To the west, you reach the mountain resort of Semenic by way of a winding road to Văliug and thence by a chairlift to the rim of the Semenic plateau.

The farther south, the better the landscape becomes, and the lush scenery of Băile Herculane and the Cazane Gorges of the Danube (which include the Iron Gates) can have few rivals in any part of the world. Horse-drawn gypsy caravans still rumble through the defiles of these forest-clad mountains as they have always done, though their number has greatly diminished since the Second World War when the Nazis hunted them down like game. For centuries the plight of this tenacious race should have troubled the consciences of all the peoples of Europe. Yet little over a century ago, if a strange gypsy dared show his face in Bohemia he would part with one of his ears; a second offence would endanger the other ear, and a third promised the removal of the head itself. In the Romanian principalities they fared little better for, since their arrival in the early Middle Ages from the east (and comparative studies have proven that their language, for all its variations, goes back to northern India), the gypsies lived as slaves or outlaws, the luckier among them managing to flee to the inaccessible fastnesses of Transylvania where, as troglodytes, they made their homes in caves formerly occupied by bears. In Transylvania the modern basket-maker or *rudar* may still be referred to as a 'man of the woods'. Today most Romanian gypsies are more or less sedentary but the nomadic urge in them, if occupations are any guide, seems by no means to be extinct. Thus many are tinkers, horse-dealers, musicians and basket-makers. The *ursari*, exhibitors of performing bears, are a frequent sight at the country fairs. It is here worth noting that the English description of the gypsy tongue as Romany has nothing whatever to do with 'Romania', for the Romany word *rom* quite simply means 'man'.

The celebrated spa of Băile Herculane is a destination for many who travel a good deal further than a gypsy even in his lifetime. Scarcely a region of Romania is without thermal springs and to a Romanian there is nothing eccentric in spending a short holiday amidst the bath, fountains and villas of an Eforie, Sovata, Govora or Băile Herculane. As naturally and seriously as the Finns take to their *sauns*, so do Romanians, the firm and infirm alike, flock to the beautiful settings of their health resorts, and to an Englishman hardly aware of Harrogate, to the American ignorant of Hot Springs, bathing here *en famille* should be at least a tonic innovation. Băile Herculane might prove the best of possible choices, for it is a resort enfolded within the most sumptuous Valley of the

Cerna, blessed by so temperate a climate that lilac often blooms twice a year.

Because the province is sheltered from the snowstorms which rage over the Wallachian Plain and equally from the wet Adriatic winds blowing across Yugoslavia, a luxuriant vegetation grows wild upon the hillsides. On the limestone ridge of Mt. Domogled towering above the spa you can find one of the richest flora in Europe. In the Domogled Nature Reserve Mediterranean, Asiatic, Alpine and endemic species such as the Banat black pine with its umbrella-shaped crown, vie for breathing space; one plant which goes by the Latin name of *saxifraga rocheliana* (meaning 'stone-breaker') is so pressed for room that it thrusts its body into any available cleft, growing and developing in grim struggle with the rock. The tenderness of the 'stone-breaker's' appearance, for it has delicate white flowers, belies its strength.

Equally prolific are the lepidoptera, and until recently Băile Herculane, with more than one thousand species, was the most famous spot in Europe for collecting butterflies. One of the commonest of these is the *coenonympha leander*, a small butterfly with powdered wings, the colour of yellow mother-of-pearl. It is easily found – and caught – on its favourite flower, the shepherd's thyme, on which it settles, refusing to budge even when assailed by human hands. Insects abound and there is one large beetle, the *procrustes gigas*, which emerges only at night, when it feasts upon snails. Near the railway station there is a notice warning tourists of snakes; two of these, the adder and horned viper are indeed venomous but they have only claimed three lives in the last one hundred years. A more interesting species is the *elaphe longissima*, a big snake which the peasants call dragon on account of its uncommon length. An impressive but harmless creature, it became the object of a cult among the Romans, who even introduced it into their towns.

It was, naturally enough, Roman colonists who first appreciated the restorative value of the countless springs bubbling from the valley floor and they were quick to dedicate the most therapeutic of these to Hercules, Aesculapius and Hygeia, naming the entire complex *Ad aquas Herculi sacras*. Indeed when they finally retired from Dacia in 271 A.D. the last cohorts to leave were those stationed at Băile Herculane. It is not hard to imagine them, somewhat like American G.I.s recalled from a Pacific atoll, torn between a sense of duty and the sybaritical round to which they had grown accustomed. The Roman thermae were not rediscovered for the outside world until the mid-18th century when, once again, the news about the efficacy of their waters spread far and wide. Hundreds of rheumatic patients from the north, inspired by a series of sensational cures, descended on the spa, making do with improvised shelter. The Austrian Governor of the Banat and even the Emperor Joseph II himself paid visits to what at that time must have been a most primitive settlement. After another century-long relapse into neglect and banditry, Băile Herculane re-emerged once and for all as a fashionable and productive watering place, even serving as a venue for the monarchs of Austria-Hungary, Romania and Serbia. It is now an object of a thousand daily peregrinations but you do not have to be afflicted with gastric ulcers or arteriosclerosis to test its beneficence or enjoy its environment.

The Danube, reuniting as it does all the rivers of the country, is an elemental part of national life, a recurrent *Leitmotiv* in Romanian literature and lore. It enters Romania in the south-west, from the prison of the Iron Gates which form but a part of the Cazane Gorges between Baziaş and Turnu-Severin. For ninety miles the river is immured by massive walls of rock frequently embellished with the densest foliage. The narrowest and least frequented of roads follow the course of the stream on both the Romanian and Yugoslav banks but the constant flotilla of Austrian steamers, Czech coaling barges, wide-hulled tankers from Constanţa and Odessa and sleek Yugoslav patrol launches leave one in no doubt as to which is the main artery of commerce in this region. Short of taking a boat the best vantage points on the Romanian side of the defile lie between Turnu-Severin and Moldova Veche.

It is at first surprising to find habitation along the banks, as at Orşova, Ogradena and Sviniţa until one remembers that since the beginning of history the Cazane Gorges have provided a natural corridor for trade, military invasion and migrations. Not counting Turnu-Severin, which was the Roman Drubeta, most of the Roman relics, such as the fortifications of Tricule, are to be seen on the Yugoslav bank – and like wise the medieval castle of Golubat. Steeped in legend is the lovely island of Ada Kaleh, known as Continusa to the Argonauts who claimed to discover the olive here. Like a battleship moored in midstream, Ada Kaleh is one of the very few inhabited islands of the Danube and was in the past a most desirable redoubt, as its Austrian fortress and Turkish mosque make plain.

At one point the sides of the seething torrent are no more than 500 feet apart and, except at midday, there is perpetual shadow. A lavish flora of chestnut, beech, vines, fig-trees, fluffy oaks and flowering ash climbs the steep slopes and narrow gullies and even the sheerest rock-face is, in spring, aflame with tulips, iris and lilac. The gorges are now undergoing greater change as a result of human activity than during their millenniums of natural evolution. By the early 1970's the river will have risen by more than one hundred feet and a huge storage lake will take its place; a system of dams, locks and generating stations – to harness its immense hydropower – is in the middle stages of construction by the Romanian and Yugoslav authorities. Without such rescue operations as were made on the Nubian Nile, the casualties of this technological *tour de force* would forever be submerged beneath the upstart lake, but, with characteristic feeling for the past, the Romanians have decided that the famous minaret and fortifications of Ada Kaleh shall rise again, on the island of Simian, some eighteen miles downstream.

At the eastern end of the defile stands Turnu-Severin, a busy river port and principal centre of western Oltenia. It was here that Trajan crossed the Danube with his legionaries to enter Dacia at the time of his second war against the Dacians (105–106 A.D.). Dacia was the last major European province to be absorbed into the Empire, not least because of the stout resistance shown to three successive Emperors, Domitian, Nerva and Trajan, by Decebal, the King of the Dacians. Trajan, who as a descendant of Roman settlers in Spain had travelled the length and breadth of his vast territories, found in Dacia mines and treasure which for once more than paid for his expensive campaigns. But Dacian exports to Rome were not confined to minerals; many Dacian warriors were taken prisoner to be sold at the great slave markets of Capua and Delos and others to be awarded a more terrible fate. During four months of the year 107 alone Trajan celebrated his Dacian triumph by dispatching, for the public amusement, ten thousand gladiators to the arena. A more durable spectacle is the colossal Column of Trajan in Rome whose pedestal houses the tomb-chambers of the Emperor and his wife, Plotina, and whose winding reliefs depict in microscopic detail the phases of the war against the luckless Dacians.

For all the sanguinary toll of defeat, the Dacians were to benefit from Roman rule and when the Imperial troops and administrators finally withdrew after one and a half centuries their impact on this Balkan province proved enduring. In this context Nicolae Iorga refers to the modern Romania as 'Eastern Romania' – in contradistinction to Italy, France and Iberia which formed a 'Western Romania', and it is certainly remarkable that this Romanised island or, as a 19th century French traveller called it, 'the foremost sentinel of Latin civilisation in Eastern Europe', should have remained intact in a sea of Slavs, Magyars and Turks, the only other direct descendants of Rome in the region being the Vlachs, that race of shepherds and merchants who still inhabit the hill valleys of modern Macedonia and Albania and who speak a tongue that is akin to Romanian.

At Turnu-Severin only the ruins of the abutments on each bank, one in Yugoslavia at Kladovo and the other on the outskirts of Turnu-Severin, remain to mark the site of the stupendous bridge built here by Trajan's architect, Apollodor of Damascus, by which the legions crossed the Danube. Above the bridge, on the open terrace of the bluff behind the modern town, are the remains of the Roman fortress of Drubeta, possibly conceived before the actual reduction of Dacia and still guarded like a bridgehead after the Roman evacuation. A visit to the Iron Gates Museum (Muzeul Porţilor de Fier), with its multiple inscriptions, bas-reliefs, fragments, coins, arms and its fascinating model of the Roman bridge, will indicate the extent of Rome's legacy. The Iron Gates hydroelectric scheme of our day is perhaps the only natural successor to the monuments of Roman engineers in the region, with the possible exception of the bridge with Constantine the Great erected at Celei in the early 4th century.

Stretched between the Banat and the River Olt curving southwards to join the Danube lies the province of Oltenia, a meeting-place of the warm westerly wind from the Mediterranean known as the 'empty wallet' and the chilly *crivaţ* which brings flurries of snow in late spring from the Russian steppe. It is curious that while 'Wallachia' is an historically impeccable term, it is now rarely referred to in everyday parlance. 'Oltenia' on the other hand, never an independent state and often named 'Little Wallachia' on account of its contributions to Wallachian culture, has assumed the full personality of a separate province. The Oltenian monasteries of Cozia and Tismana are the most ancient and venerable of Orthodox shrines in Romania and the fabulous monastery at Hurez is the finest flower of the Wallachian Renaissance. In the mountain of Oltenia characteristic forms of architecture survive in the 17th-century *cula* manor houses as at Curtişoara and Măldăreşti. These were hill dwellings built on

13. Peleş Castle at Sinaia.

15. The Prahova Valley, highway to the East.

14. *left:* A view of the Olt Valley.

16. The Bicaz Gorges in the Oriental Carpathians.

raised foundations with decorated staircases and balconies, all fortified against foes and impregnable for months at a time. Oltenians have long traditions in art. 'It is', remarks George Oprescu, 'in this land, on the very soil where the Romanian nation struck root and was nurtured that Romanian art has brought forth its most brilliant achievements. It is here that this art, which is so difficult to trace to its origins shows greatest novelty and range. A population, poor but endowed with practical gifts, perspicacity and an indefectible artistic sense has succeeded in expressing its rude but gentle soul in numberless works of unquestionable beauty.'

In all the provinces of historic Romania, from Bessarabia to the Banat, peasant women have woven carpets from time immemorial but it is in Oltenia that the art of tapestry is the most vital in its composition and most refined in colour. The borders of an Oltenian rug are usually wide, vivid and filled with a recognisable motif of animals, birds and trees; sometimes it forms a garland of brilliant flowers observed, no doubt, by their peasant creator in the course of her daily life. But the centre is equally rich in still or living themes subjected to the hyponotic rigidity of a geometrical pattern. Romanian tapestries may on occasion reflect Persian and oriental influences but one is struck not so much by these as by the remarkable, and entirely coincidental, affinities that some of them suggest with the exuberant folk weave of the Pueblo Indians and pre-Columbian Peruvians. You may be so fortunate as to enter a peasant homestead in which tapestry is a natural component; otherwise you should seek out the carpets on display in the Village Museum of Bucharest, the Craiova Town Museum and in the major Ethnological Museum (as at Cluj), or else visit the factories at the Oltenian village of Tismana, where the ancient styles are adapted to contemporary use. Tismana is also the site of the large and magnificent 14th-century monastery built by Prince Vlaicu Basarab which, though twice detroyed by the Turks, has served over the centuries as a fortress, school and hospital,

H

and as a rendezvous for the patriots of the 1821 uprising which was led by Tudor Vladimirescu.

Not far to the east lies the manufacturing township of Tîrgu Jiu, which makes a potent claim on our interest, for, at the nearby village of Pestisani, one of the fathers of modern sculpture, Constantin Brancusi, was born in 1876. As a little shepherd boy Brancusi worked in the surrounding hills and came to know the moods of nature, the architecture of land-scape and the dependency of man on the earth. All the creation of the adult sculptor is infused with the dual forces of life and death, earth and sky, peasant tradition and human individuality. Brancusi later served his apprenticeship with a local carpenter and then took up studies at the Bucharest Academy of Fine Arts where he performed his exercises so brilliantly that one of his first nude studies was acquired by the Bucharest Medical School as an anatomical model. In 1902 the impecunious young man set out on foot for Paris, where he enrolled as a student of the École des Beaux Arts and exhibited work which soon came to the attention of Rodin, who asked him to join his studio. Brancusi, rejecting the realism of European sculpture since the Renaissance and inhibited by a natural reserve which made him one of the most enigmatic of men, declined the invitation and, subsisting on his earnings as a dishwasher, embarked upon his solitary but swiftly successful career.

For Brancusi the nature of the artist's material determined the sculpture. Hence the resilience of the raw material dictated a formalism that marked a gradual break with accepted tradition, especially in human anatomy. Conventionally trained at the Beaux Arts though he was, his Head of a Child (1908) in marble was only superficially Rodinesque and, in fact, foreshadowed the highly original style of 'direct carving', penetrating to the very core of the material, which the sculptor elaborated over the next decade. If you ever visit the Cimetière Montparnasse in Paris you will be astonished to find amongst the usual slabs and crosses one small headstone that appears oddly optimistic. This is 'The Kiss', a limestone block with a stylised purity calling to mind African primitive and pre-Columbian forms, breathing not the carnal sensuality of Rodin's work but the immortal innocence of a man and woman in so tight an embrace that their very eyes are touching. And in details such as the girl's hair you detect a pattern reminiscent of an Oltenian peasant weave. 'The Kiss' was carved in 1908 as a memorial to a deceased friend. In these same years Brancusi made more lasting acquaintances, with Marcel Duchamp, Modigliani and Ezra Pound. One of his closest friends was Henri Rousseau and when the Douanier died, it was Brancusi who carved his tombstone.

Ever moved by the countryside and preoccupied with the cycles of life, Brancusi fashioned his polished and organic shapes in stone, marble, onyx, steel and wood, into forms that were but man-made counterparts to nature herself. In his middle years, when he had been widely acclaimed in Europe and America, the artist was invited by another Oltenian, Nicolae Titulescu, to return to his birthplace and construct in a riverside garden at Tîrgu Jiu several monuments of his art. Just as Henry Moore's sculpture can adorn and complement a windswept moor, so at Tîrgu Jiu do Brancusi's sculptures – the Endless Column, the drumlike Table of Silence, the monumental stone Gate of the Kiss, the small monolithic abstracts, set off a natural setting to good advantage. The slender column in steel, soaring nearly one hundred feet like a metal totem-pole, caused quite an uproar on the day of its unveiling. The middle-class spectators who were gathered laughed aloud at what they considered nothing less than an aberration of art, and the fascist press singled out Brancusi's monuments on the Jiu as prime instances of decadent abstractionism, unrelated as they were to political purposes. But the peasants, reminded perhaps of their own folk traditions, were apparently endeared to the modern and yet enduring, half-pagan simplicity of this work. Brancusi died in 1957, at the age of eighty-one and was interred in the same Cimetière Montparnasse where they laid the Douanier so many years before.

In America the Philadelphia Museum and New York Museum of Modern Art possess the best examples of Brancusi in public hands while in Europe one is urged to travel to Romania, to the Bucharest Museum of Art which contains the marvellous 'Wisdom of the Earth' (a meditating woman in stone and latter-day fertility goddess) and other work, and to Oltenia itself, to the garden on the River Jiu and the Art Museum in Craiova where they exhibit, among other things, two bronze heads of children, a variation of 'The Kiss' and a marble 'Torso of a Woman'.

In these same years two other brilliant Romanians sought their fortunes in Paris, the Dadaist Tristan Tzara and playwright Eugène Ionesco. Tzara was a fine poet but is remembered more as the leading theorist of the Dada movement. Arriving in the French capital in 1919 Tzara, together with Marcel Duchamp, Jean Arp, Max Ernst and others subsequently shocked the public ethos with their Dada manifestoes and their exhibitions of such subjects as bicycle wheels, urinals and 'Mona Lisa's Moustache'. Like Cubo-futurism and Surrealism and all the other inconoclastic '-isms' of the early years of our century, Dadaism rather soon served its purpose, if that purpose was to ventilate the stuffy confines of academic art, an achievement without which Arp, Ernst, de Chirico and other moderns might not so readily have freed themselves from the fetters of tradition and one which makes the op and pop seem respectable if not unadventurous.

Tristan Tzar, born in 1896 in the Moldavian town of Moineşti grew up in comfortable circumstances till such time as he began his studies in Bucharest. Here he formed a life-long friendship with the Romanian poet Ion Vinea and together they entered upon their literary careers. In the middle of the First World War, Tzara fled his homeland to evade his military obligation, migrated to Zurich and then, naturally enough for those days, gravitated to Paris. More than a noisy pamphleteer, the young Romanian soon proved his poetic art in the French language. The Romanian name Tzara (*tara*) means, in translation, 'country' or the Latin *terra* and it is more than a coincidence that the Moldavian countryside should have provided him with some of his best material:

Errent dan les bois
Des mediants tziganes à la barbe de centre
Et l'on a peur quand on les croise
A l'heure où le soleil frotte sa paupière contre les sentiers

Nous irons a cheval des journées entières,
Nous ferons halte dans des auberges grises,
Là on lie beaucoup d'amitiés
Et la nuit on couche avec la fille de l'aubergiste.

His verses entitled 'Terre sur Terre' (1946) are mellifluous incantations in which the world of nature is omnipresent:

nuit de fer matin de glace
cri entouré de la flamme du silence

et toi au beau milieu du fruit ouvert du jour
qu'attends-tu où vas-tu ravine perdue
j'attends la mousse première et le cri de l'agneau
l'abeille secrète la hache dans la forêt . . . . .

There is no certainty as to the origins of the term 'Dada', but according to the plausible account of Jean Arp: 'Tristan Tzara discovered the word on 6th April, 1916, at six o'clock in the afternoon; I was present with my twelve children when for the first time Tzara uttered this word which filled us with a justifiable enthusiasm. This occurred at the Café de la Terrasse in Zürich, and I was wearing a brioche in my left nostril.'

Turning from the absurdities of Dada to the theatre of the absurd, it is notable that yet another Romanian expatriate, Eugène Ionesco, should shine in that select constellation of the Parisian avant-garde. Critic, short story-writer, more recently film-script writer and the inventive dramatist behind the surrealistic front of the 'Bald Primadonna', 'The Chairs' and 'Rhinoceros', Ionesco is a native of Slatina, a small town near the Olt which now smelts aluminium and generates thermo-electric power. Born there in 1912 and dividing his youth between Paris and the Faculty of Literature in Bucharest (where he later taught French), Ionesco is a consummate symbol of the Romanian cosmopolite, like Brancusi and Tzara, equally versed in the cultures of Romania and Western Europe, and in particular of France, for whom so many Romanians feel a natural affinity.

Craiova, the old capital of Oltenia, is, like so many towns in modern Romania, host to all kinds of industrial projects and thousands of its citizens are occupied in the vast 'Electroputere' plant which produces electric and diesel locomotives for the State railways, in the sugar refinery and other factories. At the same time there are a few interesting vestiges of the Wallachian past in Craiova, among these the 17th-century (though much restored) Church of St. Dumitru and the 18th-century House of the Oltenian Bans (Casa Băniei), both in the old pre-Brancovan Wallachian style. The Wallachian idiom is, significantly, far more ostensible in Oltenian buildings than are styles usually associated with Austro-Hungarian rule. Craiova is the cultural centre for all of Oltenia and its National Theatre, State Philharmonic Orchestra, town Museum and Art Museum are on a par with those of cities such as Jassy and Timişoara.

The floodlands to the south are flat, in winter black or white according to the weather, veridian in spring when the Jiu and lower Olt have burst their banks and in summer but a golden ocean of ripening corn. On the low marshes and sand-dunes of the Danube wild duck and other game are plentiful and human occupancy rare, an equation that results in happy conditions for the more adventurous hunter. A striking feature of this part of the Danube is the difference in height between the Romanian and Bulgarian riverbanks, the latter broken only by the occasional tributary stream but the former ever vulnerable to flooding.

Often likened in the guidebooks to the pearls of a necklace, the string of spas and monasteries along the Olt, from the narrow defile whence the river breaks through the mountain barriers of Transylvania to the southern flood-plains, is a veritable crystallisation of the heroic ages of Romanian history. Here, one says to oneself when the week-end motor traffic has dispersed, time stands still. The scenery is magnificent, especially as one approaches the narrowest neck of the valley above Cozia.

Heading northwards from the sunny vineyards of Drăgăşani, cultivated since Dacian times, the road and railway reach Govora, the most southerly of the bathing resorts in the valley, renowned for its mineral springs and the healing contents of its mud. These were discovered accidentally in the last century by oil prospectors, but the monastery of Govora, originally founded in the 15th and restored in the 18th century, was for long a centre of secular and ecclesiastic learning, endowed in 1640 with that symbol of erudition, the printing-press. The wooden hills now begin to press further in on the glistening Olt but the temptation to fork up the mountain road a few miles past the monasteries of Bistriţa and Arnota to the town of Hurez cannot be resisted, for here is the most striking of monuments, a monastery consisting of a church (1691) that stands in the centre of a spacious inner courtyard surrounded by one-storeyed buildings: a belfry, cells, refectory, chapel, prince's residence, kitchen and look-out tower, and an arched gallery leading to another cloister. The rich ornamentation, the stucco, the carved stone columns and archways, the pear-wood staircases, doors, windows and iconostasis engraved with floral, animal and mythological designs, the ravishing frescoes: these constitute the most celebrated group of Brancovan buildings in old Wallachia. Constantin Brîncoveanu, who with his family is commemorated

by portraits on the walls of the church, supervised the construction at Hurez and later retired here during the summer.
In the neighbourhood are the small but elegant 18th-century
Hermitage of St. Stephen and a ceramics works where an
ancient form of highly decorated pottery is still practised with
traditional tools.

Farther west on the highroad to Tîrgu Jiu, the fortified
manor-houses at Măldăreşti offer the best examples of those
cula structures which have already been mentioned. Built as a
protection against Turkish horsemen in the 18th and early
19th centuries, these buildings are as original a form of
fortification as the ethereal towers of Svanetian villages in the
Caucasus. One *cula* at Măldăreşti now holds a museum. Then
at Polovraci, near the dramatic gorges of the River Olteţ
which served as a refuge for *haiduks*, stands the 17th-century
monastery of Polovraci, containing splendid frescoes.

Reaching the proportions of a ravine the Valley of the Olt
enjoys the protection of its mountain walls. Dense forests of
oak and beech climb the flanks and while summers are temperate, the winters are kinder than in the rest of Oltenia and
Wallachia. The adjoining spas of Călimăneşti and Căciulata
possess thermae that are so warm that business continues
throughout the year. The old chronicles note that Voivod
Matei Basarab, ensconced in the monastery at Cozia, used
to bathe in a nearby vat which 'eased his pains', and Napoleon
III had a standing order for the mineral waters of Căciulata.
In the middle of the Olt at Călimăneşti is the island known
simply by the Slavonic word for island, 'Ostrov'. The chapel
of the 16th-century nunnery of Ostrov still survives like a
marooned ship. Only two miles upstream is the complex of
Cozia Monastery whose architectural influences on the whole
of Wallachia were inestimable. Its church first completed in
1386 by Mircea the Old, who is buried here, Cozia is the
oldest Orthodox monastery in Romania. At the same time
the stylistic impact of Byzantium was first revealed at Cozia
in façades of alternating stone and red brick and in the three-

cusped plan originating at Constantinople. The stone carvings, the 14th- and 18th-century frescoes and the portico added by Brîncoveanu in 1707 are visual delights almost without comparison. Other parts of the monastery are of interest too, in particular the Museum with its icons and the Bolniţa Church which originally adjoined the monastic hospital.

Looming above the valley to the east is Mt. Cozia on whose slopes an exotic vegetation of dog-roses, walnuts and *Edelweiss* thrives in wild abandon. An easy path leading from the Turnul Monastery (whose rock cells were occupied by monks in the 17th century) will take you to one of the loveliest of panoramas, extending from the serrated peaks of the Făgăraş to the gentle foliage of the lower Olt. And it is not difficult to appreciate the protection that the mountain bulwark of Argeş afforded the Wallachian patriots of old.

The defile of the Olt attains its scenic climax not far north of the Hermitage of Cornetu which was begun by the Ban of Craiova in 1666 and later ornamented with ceramic tiles and girded with a simple but effective outer wall. In early spring the deafening roar of the rushing river gives the sensation of a besieging army and these wonderful monasteries again become havens of solitude and contemplative ease.

Oltenia, the Banat and the other provinces of the country are on the move. The rising flood of the Danube at the Iron Gates is an incisive symbol of the titatic rearrangement of nature or, as the ideologues would say, of the harnessing of productive forces, which is the rule in modern Romania. The floodgates of tourism will open up another kind of stream and it will not be long before the glorious and singular beauties of the Romanian landscape are within reach of all.

USEFUL INFORMATION

EUROPEAN ROMANIAN
NATIONAL TOURIST OFFICES
Office National de Tourisme
1 *rue Daunou, Paris 2e, Tel.* RIC, 31–32
Romanian National Tourist Office
98–99 *Jermyn Street, London* S.W. 1
Tel. WHI*tehall* 8812–8813
Rumanisches Touristenamt
Opernring 1, *Vienna* 1010, *Tel.* 57.16.58
and 57.77.02
Romanian National Tourist Office
Norra Banttorget 29, *Stockholm* 27,
Tel. 21.02.53 *and* 21.02.63
Romanian National Tourist Office
Vesterborgade 55 A, *Copenhagen* 5, *Tel.*
EVA 6219
OfficeNational Roumain de Tourisme
26 *Place Brouchere, Brussels* 1,
Tel. 01–18.00.79 *and* 18.63.82
Office National Roumain de Tourisme
Via della Farnessina, 232–234 *Rome.*

HOW TO REACH ROMANIA
BY TRAIN: *A railway network links the
chief towns of Europe with Bucharest.*
Wiener Walzer: *Paris East – Basle –
Zürich – Vienna – Budapest –
Bucharest.* Balt Orient Express:
*Stockholm, Malmo – Berlin East –
Dresden – Prague – Bratislava –
Budapest, Episcopia Bihor – Bucharest.*
Orient Express: *Paris East – Munich –
Vienna – Budapest – Bucharest.*
Nord Orient Express: *Warsaw –
Budapest – Episcopia Bihor – Bucharest.*

Carpati Express: *Warsaw – Lvov –
Vicsani – Bucharest.*
Danubius Express: *Moscow – Kiev –
Kishinev – Ungheni – Bucharest.*
Belgrade-Bucharest: *Belgrade –
Timisoara – Craiova – Bucharest.*
Moscow-Bucharest: *Moscow – Kiev –
Ungheni – Nicolina – Jassy – Bucharest.*
Moscow-Bucharest: *Moscow – Kiev –
Ungheni – Nicolina – Jassy – Bucharest.*
Sofia-Bucharest: *Sofia – Russe –
Giurgiu – Bucharest.*
BY AIR: Tarom (*Romanian Airlines*)
*operates regular flights to Paris – Zürich –
Brussels – Frankfort – London – Rome –
Copenhagen – Vienna – Cairo – Athens –
Berlin – Belgrade – Budapest – Moscow –
Prague – Sofia – Warsaw – Amsterdam –
Beirut – Istanbul – Kiev and Zagreb.*
*Flights to and from Romania (regular
passenger services) are also operated by the
foreign companies:* Aeroflot (*USSR*)*;*
Air France (*France*)*;* AUA (*Austria*)*;*
KLM (*the Netherlands*)*;* Interflug (*the
German Democratic Republic*)*;* LOT
(*Poland*)*;* MALEV (*Hungary*)*;*
SABENA (*Belgium*)*;* BALKANAIR
(*Bulgaria*)*;* LUFTHANSA (*the
Federal Republic of Germany*)*;* Swissair
(*Switzerland*).
Băneasa International Airport *is only
8 km. from the centre of Bucharest and*
Kogălniceanu International Airport,
*which lies 30 km. from the port city of
Constanta, serves the sea coast.*

Useful Information

BY SEA: *A trip on the Danube aboard the Romanian river-going ships is very pleasant. They sail on regular cruises from May to October, on this route: Vienna, with stops at Bratislava, Budapest, Belgrade, Turnu Severin, Giurgui (for sightseeing in Bucharest) and Hirsova (from where coaches carry the tourist to the Black Sea shore.)*

FOREIGN CURRENCY EXCHANGE AND PRICES

Foreign travellers who possess a tourist visa are entitled to an exchange premium of 200% for free convertible currencies (*e.g.* US $ = 18 *lei*). Tourists may enter Romania with any amount of currency. The exchange bureaux of the National Bank of the Socialist Republic of Romania, at all frontier points and also in all urban localities, at big hotels and NTO agencies, will exchange on request any amount of currency. Letters of credit are valid in Romania. Lei remaining unspent can be changed into the tourist's native currency at any exchange office on production of the receipt giving the currency exchange he made on arrival.

Romania's currency unit is the '*leu*' with its sub-division the '*ban*': *1 leu* = 100 *bani*. The banknotes are of 100 *lei*' 50 *lei*, 25 *lei*, 10 *lei*, 5 *lei*, 3 *lei* and 1 *leu*, and coins – 3 *lei*, 1 *leu*, 25 *bani*, 15 *bani*, 10 *bani*, and 5 *bani*.

The shops are open every day morning and afternoon, closed Sundays and national holidays. Department stores are open all day in Bucharest and in other big towns, and de luxe and highclass category restaurants are open daily, from 8 *a.m.* in the morning to 2 *a.m.* the next morning. Night clubs are open from 10 *p.m.* to 4 *a.m.*

In large towns there are special shops selling such articles as handicrafts, records, drinks, souvenirs (with payment in foreign currency or travellers' cheques earning a 20% reduction on sales-prices).

Postal charges for abroad differ in Romania according to the category of the mail. A picture postcard – 1 *leu*; ordinary letter – 1.60 *leu*; registered letter – 4 *lei*; express registered letter – 7.20 *lei*.

Examples of prices are: 1 *kg.* meat from 10 to 28 *lei*; 1 *kg.* sugar – 9 *lei*; 1 *kg.* edible oil – 11 *lei*; 1 *kg.* white bread – 4.40 *lei*; 1 *kg.* halfwhite bread – 3.20 *lei*; 1 *kg.* brown bread – 2 *lei*; 1 packet of 20 Snagov cigarettes – 8 *lei*; 1 packet of Litoral cigarettes – 5 *lei*; 1 packet of Carpati cigarettes – 2.50 *lei*; 1 box of marches – 0.20 *lei*.

MOTORING

There is no special entry procedure nor any custom or traffic tax for motorists who come to Romania. Motoring tourists need only an international or national driving licence for the vehicle they are driving. In Romania the 'passage-en-douane' carnets type AIT or FIA are valid; for those who do not possess them, it is enough to be provided with the national 'passage-en-douane' carnet, acknowledged by Romania through the bilateral agreements, or a temporary import-export permit. A 'Green Card' is also necessary. Motoring tourists can cross the frontier into Romania at any time, both day and night, as the customs and currency exchange offices are permanently open (inclusive of holidays). The NTO bureaux at frontier points and in the main towns provide any information and services you may require. Petrol and oil prices are as follows: Petrol 75 octane: 1.45 *lei/litre*; petrol 90 actane: 1.70 *lei/litre*; petrol 90 octane: 1.90 *lei/litre*; +5 Diesel oil: 0.42 *lei/litre*; oil 5.90: 15.70 *lei/litre*.

There are Peco filling stations in most towns and at intervals of from 50 to 100 *km.* along main roads. The Peco stations are generally open for 15 hours (7 *a.m.* to 10 *p.m.*). There are special garages in big towns open 24 hours a day. The main roads of Romania are served by the yellow cars of ACR (*Automobile Club – Romania*) which make running repairs and replace parts. ACR of Bucharest (27 *Nikos Beloianis Street*) is affiliated to FIA and FIC; it provides any kind of information and legal and technical assistance.

Permitted Maximum Speed

	Built-up areas	Open areas
Cars	60 *km/h*	100 *km/h*
Motorcycles	40 *km/h*	60 *km/h*
Coaches	40 *km/h*	80 *km/h*

In Romania traffic is on the right side of the road.

Traffic Lights: The green light is for vehicles to drive on or to turn right or left, and for pedestrians to cross the street. The amber light means that vehicles must stop at intersections. The red light stops traffic from driving in intersections. The intermittent amber light requires motorists to slow down in order to avoid risks and at the same time to ascertain they can proceed without interfering with traffic at intersections.

Traffic Officer's Signs: The traffic officer indicates 'stop' for vehicles and pedestrians coming from in front with the left arm vertically raised and the palm turned forward; for vehicles and pedestrians coming from behind with the right arm and the palm horizontally extended. These signs can be made simultaneously; the traffic officer can signal by hand to the vehicles to drive on, to pass in front or behind him, turning left or right or to pedestrians to cross the street.

Priority: When two vehicles get simultaneously close to an inter-section, coming from roads devoid of priority signposts at intersections, priority is given to the vehicle arriving from the right. Priority is also given to the vehicle driving on a section of road at whose beginning there is the 'Priority road' or 'Right of way over oncoming' sign post, or this priority is maintained at an intersection at whose beginning is the signpost 'Inter-section without priority'. Traffic signals expected from the driver are the same as in most European countries, including the UK.

Readers are recommended to a complete and concise book with much additional information. It is called ROMANIA: A COMPLETE GUIDE and is published at 25s. by GARNSTONE PRESS, 59 *Brompton Road, London* s.w.3.

SELECT BIBLIOGRAPHY

T. Appleton, *Your Guide to Rumania*, London, 1965

G. Balan, *George Enescu*, 1962

S. Cioculescu and others, *Romania: A Guidebook*, Bucharest, 1967

Institut de Archeologie, *Dacia-Revue d'Archéologie*, Bucharest

N. Iorga, *Histoire des Roumains*, Paris, 1937

I. Jianou, *Brancusi*, London/Paris, 1963

P. Latham, *Romania: A Complete Guide*, Garnstone Press, London, 1967

M. Mackintosh, *Rumania*, London, 1963

Nagel Travel Series, *Rumania*, Geneva/Paris/Munich, 1967

G. Oprescu, *Peasant Art in Roumania*, London, 1929

G. Oprescu and A. Crabar, *Painted Churches of Moldavia*, New York, 1963

E. Pop and N. Salageanu, ed., *Nature Reserves in Romania*, Bucharest, 1965

R. W. Seton-Watson, *A History of The Roumanians from Roman Times to The Completion of Unity*, Cambridge, 1934

W. Starkie, *Raggle-Taggle: Adventures with a Fiddle in Hungary and Roumania*, London, 1948

L. S. Stavrianos, *The Balkans since 1453*, New York, 1958

T. Tzara, *Les Premiers Poèmes*, Paris, 1965

R. L. Wolff, *The Balkans in Our Times*, Oxford, 1916

B. I. Jamset, *Basic Rumanian*, London, 1950

G. Nandris, *Colloquial Rumanian*, London, 1966

G. O. Seiver, *Introduction to Romanian*, New York, 1953

Also helpful are the general and regional pocket guides (in English) issued by the Meridiane Publishing House, Bucharest.

INDEX

Index